REFLECTIONS ON REASON, RELIGION, AND TOLERANCE

REFLECTIONS ON REASON, RELIGION, AND TOLERANCE:

Engaging with Fethullah Gülen's Ideas

Klas Grinell

New York

Published by Blue Dome Press
244 5th Avenue, Suite D-149
New York, NY 10001, USA

www.bluedomepress.com

Library of Congress Cataloging-in-Publication Data
Grinell, Klas.
Reflections on reason, religion, and tolerance : engaging with Fethullah Gülen's ideas
/ Klas Grinell.
pages cm
Includes index.
ISBN 978-1-935295-56-3 (alk. paper)
1. Gülen, Fethullah. 2. Tolerance--Religious aspects--Islam. 3. Faith and reason--Islam.
4. Islamic ethics. 5. Gülen Hizmet Movement. I. Title.
BP80.G8G75 2015
297.5'699--dc23
2014037368

ISBN: 978-1-935295-56-3

Printed by
Imak Ofset, Istanbul - Turkey

Contents

Introduction

I n the spring of 2008 a poll to name the world's top intellectual was organized by the magazines Foreign Policy and Prospect. Over half a million persons gave their vote on internet. The winner was Fethullah Gülen, a Turkish preacher living in the USA.

The poll organizers were surprised and confused—as was the rest of the world. Who was this Gülen? How could he come in ahead of established intellectuals like Umberto Eco or Noam Chomsky? As a matter of fact, all of the top ten intellectuals in the poll come from the Muslim world, and at least half of them work within the Muslim tradition. The magazine's presentation of the result opened with a discussion of the difficulties in ranking intellectual strength and impact. Most Western newspapers that reported the results talked about a Muslim mobilization, as if some kind of cheating had taken place. No one seemed to be able to imagine that the easiest explanation of the result was that Gülen was in fact a top intellectual. In 2014, there was another poll, where almost no Muslim names were even on the list of nominees, as if the organizers wanted to keep it a Western, secular affair; as if Muslims did not belong among the top intellectuals.

I was happy to see the result, happy that the Muslims who topped the list were persons far from fundamentalism, violence and the stuff that in mainstream media often seems portrayed as the core of Islam.

Islam, reason and tolerance... For many this seems to be a surprising line of words. This is the one fact that convinced me to finally write this book. On one level my book is about something quite specific; the writings of the Turkish Islamic preacher and thinker Fethullah Gülen, and his representations of Islam. In talking about something specific and limited the book also speaks about what Islam really is. What *one* specific representation of Islam really is. That is the only way we can understand what Islam really is: by making one plus one plus one specific representation of how Islam can be understood and lived. The sum of all of these very different representations is what makes up that what we call Islam, what many would rather talk about as Islams, to emphasize its plurality and differences.[1] Like any other great system of thought and belief one can find support for almost any view and position in Islam. The variability and difference in what can count as Islamic is vast and expansive.[2]

The result of the top intellectual poll indicates that a huge number of people are inspired by Gülen and other Muslim intellectuals. It also shows that people other than the classical Western intellectuals are an important force in the world. The result is a clear sign of a new global public sphere that we all need to get used to and adapt to. Those that want to take part in this global public sphere would be wise to learn more about what engages thinkers from perspectives different than their own.

I like Islam. I find many beautiful, intriguing and breathtaking traditions and practices in Islam. And of course there is, as in any tradition, a lot of authoritarianism, male dominance, insularism and complacency also in Muslim communities. Still I believe in the positive power of Islam, that Islam can be a vital part in a positive societal development.

Others, not least in my native Sweden, are critical of religion as such. This is most often a valid and peace seeking stance. Critiques of religion, and any other system of thought, are important, and often very valid. It is always important to question what we see as normal. In Sweden, where I come from and live, we have a public debate that often

---

[1]   A classical and important book from this perspective is Aziz al-Azmeh, *Islams and Modernities* (New York: Verso, 1993).

[2]   Omid Safi, (red.) *Progressive Muslims: On Justice, Gender and Pluralism* (Oxford: Oneworld Publications, 2003). See also Scott Siraj al-Haqq Kugle, *Homosexuality in Islam: Critical Reflections on Gay, Lesbian, and Transgender Muslims* (Oxford: Oneworld Publications, 2010); Kecia Ali, *Sexual Ethics and Islam: Feminist Reflections on the Qur'an, Hadith and Jurisprudence* (Oxford: Oneworld Publications, 2006); Fatima Mernissi, *The Veil and the Male Elite: A Feminist Interpretation of Women's Rights in Islam* (New York: Basic Books, 1992); Farid Esack, *On Being a Muslim: Finding a Religious Path in the World Today* (Oxford: Oneworld Publications, 2009).

seems to take for granted that a thinking, reflective person cannot be religious. It is considered more evolved and mature to have seen through religious fantasies about invisible creatures and life after death. This is the context of my experiences. I think that it is important to point it out. Normality is very contextual, and the North European, Scandinavian, Swedish context is quite different from the context of the United States and many other larger countries. I have felt at home in this secularized and partly socialist outlook, and have taken it pretty much for granted. I still identify with the left and with critical theory even if I have come to feel that secularization and urbanization has left us without strong social rituals and means to express our need for belonging and trust. It has been important for me to try to honestly engage with religious perspectives to understand what role they could and should have in my life and in our society.

The sociological theory of modernization, and the included idea of secularization, held that religion would disappear as societies got modern and the inhabitants thereby became rational. This has not happened. Very few countries ever fitted in this model, even if Sweden happened to be one of those few. Today we see a return of religion and religiosity even in our country, and in most parts of the world religion have always been a strong and inexorable part of the lives of peoples and states. One can wish that this wasn't the case; one may even argue that it would be better if this weren't the case. But to think that being an atheist is the result of some historical necessity and that one therefore are more advanced than those who practice religion is an expression of an ideological modernism that no longer holds sway.

As philosopher, feminist and queer theorist Judith Butler puts it:

> If religions functions as a key matrix for the articulation of values, and if most people in this global condition look to religion to guide their thinking on such matters, we would make a political error in claiming that religion ought to be overcome in each and every instance.[3]

---

[3]   Judith Butler, *Frames of War: When is Life Grievable?* (New York: Verso, 2009) 122.

As more and more researchers are acknowledging the fact that politics and societies are not secularized, the question arises if also social theory might reinterpret its relation to religious traditions.

Post-secularity seems to entail a growing interest in ethics, in the use of knowledge, in the need for reflection, and in the recognition of the fundamental relational character of all knowledge, of life. This shift from "objective" knowledge towards a more relational understanding can be traced in many different fields.

According to a prominent strand of political philosophy, the ultimate aim of politics is to strive towards the best possible form of community. A good life and a prosperous society, according to many in the positivistic strand of what we can call the Enlightenment tradition, could be reached by replacing faith and irrationalism for objective facts and positive knowledge.

The world does not consist of facts to be observed. The world is always being rebuilt through relationships, and thus we cannot produce a space from which to observe the world objectively. The things we try to understand, and we ourselves, are always already reworked in a productive relationship with ourselves.

The world is constantly rebuilt by agency. And agency is everywhere, not only connected to intellects. Since the intra-connectedness of agents is what shapes the world, there is no study of the world disconnected from ethics. Karen Barad writes: "Ethics is about accounting for our part of the entangled webs we weave."[4] Our prime goal cannot be to know objects as accurately as possible; it must instead be to take responsibility for our relationship with the world.

Human knowledge is always partial and situated; to see more, we need to engage with more than one way of approaching the world. Swedish philosopher Mats Rosengren describes doxology as a need to multiply and shatter our focus to see the world differently—to squint with the eyes and resist the attempts towards systematic exposition.

---

[4]   Barad, Karen *Meeting the Universe Halways: Quantum Physics and the Entanglement of Matter and Meaning.* (Duke University Press, 2007) 384.

This relational responsibility that might be one aspect of post-secularity calls for a broader reflection on our relation to the world, Being, the Universe, wholeness (*tawhid*), God.

While in the 1970s most resistance movements in the Muslim world were socialist, today many of them are Islamist, and frighteningly, many have a militant and violent agenda. At the same time, the extremists comprise only a few per million of the total Muslim population of the world. Most Muslims in the world have never ever been part of any resistance movement. But somehow the militants have managed to become the emblematic image of Islam; many in the West believe that Islam is a warlike, intolerant religion. This book is part of a counter force that wants to show that Islam has more often been a peaceful, tolerant religion. What we are experiencing is not a Muslim problem, an issue with Islam; the problem is that certain representations of Islam get paid too much attention—within the religion, as well as externally. The concrete example often chosen to represent contemporary Islam is somewhat arbitrary. The most important thing is to start recognizing the plurality of alternative Islams.

Fethullah Gülen's representations of Islam have a significant following in the world today, not least in Turkey, but also in other parts of the world. Gülen is not one of the most progressive interpreters of Islam; there are many interesting feminist theologians, queer theologians and liberation theologians of other kinds in the house of Islam. Gülen is more traditional. He considers Islam to be the straightest path to more peace and tolerance in the world today. His traditional and contemporary representation of Islam motivates millions of people in the world to engage in social work, building schools and promoting dialogue. If more people in Sweden, the US and other Western counties knew that this is also what we can learn from Islam, we might also become more accepting and open towards the Muslim world.

As said, this book is about Fethullah Gülen and Turkish Islam. In presenting Gülen's thinking and the context from which it arises I want to build a space for other representations of, and positions on, Islam. There is a great need for this, not the least in the tense contemporary European climate where more and more people are looking for scapegoats and the public debate on Islam is too often portrayed as divided between Islamophobes and dictator-loving halal hippies.

What's more, I also claim that Islam is not only something to learn about, but that Islam also is something to learn *from* and be part of, as a rich tradition and civilization, even for those that do not want to take a stand on the question of faith.

Even if I am not a practicing Muslim, I will allow myself to take Fethullah Gülen's ideas with such seriousness that I also object when I meet thoughts that I cannot make sense of, cannot include in my idea of a good and just society. But, and this is very important—it is not about measuring his values against mine, measuring Islam against the West. I am more interested in opening a dialogue where respect is both given and taken. I will try to listen very closely and attentively to Gülen and the arguments of other Muslims, and I will also demand space for my own arguments, for values that are central in my life.

I would like us to think and explore together. I will share my thoughts and try to show how I have been engaged and affected by my subject. This is more disclosing and personal (perhaps even egocentric) than what is common in most books on Islam, but along the way I will do my best to explain and show the value of this approach.

Among Gülen's extensive writings we find a broad four volume discussion of key concepts in the practice of Sufism. One of these central concepts is reflection (*tafakkur* in Arabic). To reflect is to think deeply on a subject—systematically and in detail. Such reflections are, according to Gülen's poetic way of expression, "the heart's lamp, the soul's food, the spirit of knowledge, and the essence and light of the Islamic way of life."[5] Deep and repeated reflection produces a sound relation to the world, he says. Through reflection we can read the Universe as a book, we can study, and learn from, everything around us. And we must not see the world as merely something to master and use—the knowledge we can reach in reflection should be a source of reverence, humility and love for the Creator, says Gülen.

---

[5]   M. Fethullah Gülen, *Emerald Hills of the Heart: Key Concepts in the Practice of Sufism*, vol. 1, (New Jersey: The Light, 2004) 10.

The sciences are mere tools, the knowledge they produce are the building blocks for reflection. The goal according to Gülen is always to try to attain knowledge of God. Still, scientific methods are vital, for it is only when we have gotten to know and understand all the wondrous details of creation that we can reflect correctly on God's greatness and be awakened to a real love of God. The one that is content with only scientific knowledge will never know the world fully, says Gülen. He is thus a representative of a classical Islamic epistemology.

My book is a reflection on what my knowledge about, and experience of, Islam means; it is an attempt at Sufi *tafakkur*. I will not, however, address the question of God's existence. Whatever one's views and doubts, we all have something to learn from religious reflections. This might be even more important to stress in a Scandinavian setting where atheism or agnosticism is the social standard. The reluctance to talk about God finds support in Prophet Muhammad, who said that "No act of worship is as meritorious as reflection. So reflect on God's bounties and the works of His Power, but do not try to reflect on His Essence, for you will never be able to do that."[6]

I will not go into these impossible reflections on God's Essence, but rather confine myself to reflections over creation and how we can accept its bounties in a way that does not produce strife or destruction.

What is the purpose of knowledge? What good is it to us? I believe Gülen is right when he stresses that reflection must lead us beyond scientific facts and technological utility to some kind of relationship to the world, ecology, creation, God (or whatever we feel comfortable calling the totality that is grander than our utility and horizon.)

This book is a result of academic, scientific work. I am a humanistic researcher and what I write is grounded in humanistic methods and theories. At the same time, I have listened enough to my object of study to see the need to reflect in the results of my research. This is why the text sometimes strays from the conventions of academic writing.

The people inspired by Gülen are often called the Gülen (or Hizmet) Movement. They are a contested movement. For a long time, they were

---

[6] Gülen, *Emerald Hills of the Heart*, vol. 1, 10.

seen as working almost in tandem with the Justice and Development Party (Adalet ve Kalkınma Partisi, AK Party) in transforming Turkey from a staunch secularist state into a democracy with more room for Muslim sentiments. After the elections in 2011, an increasing rift could be seen between the AK Party and the Movement. This burst into a full-blown conflict in 2013, when Prime Minister Recep Tayyip Erdoğan first accused Gülen of having a role in the Gezi protests, and intensified in the new year, when the Prime Minister claimed that the Movement fabricated a graft probe to topple his government, calling them enemies of the Turkish state.

This book goes to print in the midst of a very tense situation. Where this conflict will lead, I do not know. It might be important to note, though, that my reflections are not so much on the Gülen Movement as on the message of Fethullah Gülen. This is a more stable matter, even if the interpretations might change in the future. I have tried to bring the manuscript up to date, even if its main narrative is set before this turbulence took off.

By the way, the list of the world's top living intellectuals read like this:[7]

1. Fethullah Gülen
2. Muhammad Yunus
3. Yusuf al-Qaradawi
4. Orhan Pamuk
5. Aitzaz Ahsan
6. Amr Khaled
7. Abdolkarim Soroush
8. Tariq Ramadan
9. Mahmood Mamdani
10. Shirin Ebadi

---

[7] The list can hopefully still be found at www.prospectmagazine.co.uk/2008/07/intellectualstheresults/

Chapter 1

My First Meeting with
the Gülen Movement

E arly nineties. Afyon, a tiny and insignificant little Turkish city on the Anatolian highland, known to have the best *lokum* pastries in the country, the best makers of Turkish delight. The flat city is dominated by a castle on a dramatic cliff, a cliff that I unfortunately never have had the time to climb. The castle is situated in the western outskirts of town, above blocks of old, worn down houses in beautiful pastel colors that could just as well have been found on some Greek island in the Aegean Sea. Among the old houses on the mountain rim lies an old Seljuk mosque from the late 13th century. It shares similarities with the Andalusian grand mosque of Cordoba, which in its turn has traces of the tent mosques that were used in very early Islamic times. Inside, rows upon rows of pillars form a forest, a filled space where there is room for many people.

The mosque in Afyon is a local mosque, humble and filled with rough carpets, even if it is called the Grand mosque. Well, anyway, this is not supposed to be a handbook of Islamic architecture, nor a Turkish travelogue.

But I did work as a tour guide in Turkey, then, in the early nineties. One night a week I stayed with my tourist groups in Afyon, on the road from Pamukkale to İstanbul. After lunch, one day in the end of May 1993, I had shown the old mosque to a group of Scandinavian tourists. Now they had some time on their own to stroll around and enjoy the quiet rural town life, to watch the wood carvers which are the city's biggest pride next to the *lokum* manufacturers.

At the main intersection in Afyon, where the old and the new town meet, at the tea garden next to the big war memorial, I sat this afternoon with Emel Öz and drank black tea in tulip glasses, and we talked, in English. It was still a bit cool here on the Anatolian plateau, still pleasant to sit in the sun.

Emel, who had grown up in Manavgat on the south coast, used to work for our local tour operator. Now she was on her way to İstanbul to begin her studies at the university, and had hitched a ride with our tour bus. As we sat there in the sun on our tiny plastic chairs, talking, a small, neat, intense boy came up to us. He was very keen to practice his English. I think I remember that his name was Ali. He was eleven or twelve and after a while we understood that he lived in a dormitory run by the followers of Fethullah Gülen. This was in 1993 and I did not understand much of what this meant. Emel was concerned that he was under religious influences there and that he was being trained for a "predefined role" in society, which made me wonder. Emel herself had left a quite traditionalistic and patriarchal small town in order to get a better education, and to explore opportunities with the expectation to be exposed to different ways of life and different cultures. She knew her hometown was not able to offer all this despite the influence the tourism industry had already had. She realized after many years that this education she was so keen on was something that not every female member of the Manavgat community would have the right to pursue.

Anyway, I thought I ought to find out more about this movement or organization that with promises of good education lured young boys into Islamic schools. But I soon forgot my intention and didn't think further about it for some years.

Later I came to understand that this little conversation in the tea garden in Afyon was my very first encounter with the movement that has come to engage me more and more. This boy that might have been called Ali went to a school run by people often known as the community of the Gülen Movement, or *Hizmet Hareketi*—hard working Muslims inspired by the preaching and pedagogics of Fethullah Gülen. In the schools inspired by Gülen students study hard, focusing on English and science. The teachers are Muslims, but rather than teaching about

Islam they are role models and supposed to inspire the students to become good persons.

The people inspired by Gülen do not like being called *Fethullahcı*'s. The –"ci" ending often translates into English as –"ist" and has a negative ring in the Turkish language, associated with reactionary movements, like the 'ist' in Islamist. For example, *tarikatçı* means "sectarian" in Turkish, even if the word *tarikat* is the word denoting what we most often call Sufi orders. Gülen insists that he does not have any movement. There are of course people that are inspired by him, but Gülen does not lead them in any order or sect. Gülen does speak about a movement of individuals featuring good virtues and who do their best to be exemplary citizens (*temsil*) rather than preach (*tebliğ*). Those engaged in the movement most often talk about doing service (*hizmet*), i.e. to participate in social work and mobilize others to do so, and this is considered as a means to attain God's good pleasure. It is a commitment, rather than membership.

There are now over one thousand schools worldwide that are part of the movement that takes its inspiration from the message of Fethullah Gülen. Many are still in Turkey, but new ones are constantly opening in every part of the world. In the USA there are some Gülen-inspired schools, and there is even one private school in Stockholm, Sweden. There are a few recently published good books about this movement available in English. My own interest and expertise is not centered on the movement, even if it represents a quite remarkable example of rapid and global grassroots mobilization. My expertise lies in writing texts about texts.

One of the most recent books about the movement is Joshua D. Hendrick's *Gülen: The ambiguous politics of market Islam in Turkey and the World*. It is promoted as the first dispassionate study of the Gülen Movement. Most other fuller studies are either done by people supporting the movement, or by people out to portray them as a danger. Hendrick have done extensive ethnographic field work and gives a fantastic breath of organizational detail on companies and organizations affiliated with the movement. His main point is to show how well coordinated different initiatives in various areas such as education, media, dialogue institutes and business are. This is the work of a dedicated movement. There are few links of ownership or other formal partnerships between different companies and organizations, though. This explains why specific schools or organizations often say that they have no formal ties to the Gülen Movement and that they are free enterprises, something that is formally true. Especially in the US there has been a strong debate on the charter schools started by Hizmet affiliates. They followed the usual practice of not promoting themselves as "Gülen schools" and in response to direct questions denied that they were part of any movement. Hendrick says that this is quite understandable from a Turkish perspective where openly acting as a movement have been illegal and dangerous. What he calls "the politics of ambiguity" has been a matter of survival and should not be judged as being secretive or as a proof of any hidden agenda, even if it is also understandable that it might make people suspicious about why something that seems obvious is not stated openly. I think this logic is at work also among secularists in Turkey and that it might be something for the movement's volunteers to re-evaluate.

Some people have wanted to use Hendrick as proof that the Gülen Movement is fishy. He never says they are. But his chosen theoretical focus on political and economic mobilization sometimes makes his language a bit harsh. For example, he consistently talks about all dialogue activities and publishing as "GM public relations," and his focus is exclusively on how they function to legitimize GM-affiliated schools and business. Even if dialogue and publishing most probably do function as PR, it is one-sided to call it only that. From a broader theoretical perspective than the one Hendrick has worked with, there is no contradiction in sincerely believing a message of peace and dialogue and succeeding in the business world. In everything but very minor details, I find nothing in Hendrick's analysis to argue with, within the frame of his theoretical perspective. What is important to stress is that there are other important perspectives which can also address intentions. Regarding Hendrick's assertion that the movement only supports business interest, these other perspectives make his terminology seem not only dispassionate, but at times insinuative. Hendrick is also unlucky in that his research was made in a period where there was a lot of mutual coordination between Hizmet and the AK Party. It will be very interesting to see how he will address Erdoğan's choice of Hizmet as one of his main enemies. I think it would be cheap to use this new turn against Hendrick's analysis. Most probably, it supports what most of my friends in the movement say: *It is not us who have changed.* On the question as to whether the Gülen Movement is a political movement, I will have more to say in the last chapter of this book. I want to stress this again: This book is a reflection mainly on Fethullah Gülen's writings and not on the political, social, and economic impact of the Hizmet Movement. It is more about what I have learned from Gülen than what people within the movement are inspired to do. It is also published by a company that Hendrick counts as engaged in public relations for the movement. What Hendrick's perspective might miss is that communications and dialogue are working both ways. In my experience, the people of the movement are serious readers and I am happy to engage with them in this context and hope to share thoughts so that we can influence each other to the better.

Anyway, back to the schools. The Gülen schools do not have an Islamic agenda or curriculum. In each country they follow the local school regulations and curricula and focus on language, science and math. If anything, the schools appear to promote Turkish nationalism, as some students study Turkish and along with the local national anthem the Turkish national anthem is sometimes sung. At the Turkish Language Olympiads over 500 young students from over 110 countries recite Turkish poems, sing Turkish songs and dance Turkish folk dances in front of large audiences in the largest congress halls in Turkey. The Turkish Language Olympiads is one good example of how the Gülen Movement works. This competition is organized by the Turkish cultural and educational ministries, in cooperation with the Turkish language association and the nationalistic organization *Türk Ocakları*, among others. This service-oriented Hizmet Movement is a network of dedicated persons inspired by Gülen and each other to work hard and invest money in activities they think strengthen their ideals. Even if the language Olympiads is used to be state-sponsored event (until the government started accusing Hizmet), the reporting and interest in it is most detailed in Gülen-inspired media sources. Without the Hizmet schools worldwide there would not be many participants in the competitions. So, it has not been that easy to keep state interests, commercial interests and Gülen interests apart. There does not seem to be any contradictions between the Turkish, the Islamic, the Western and the European in Gülen's thought.

The US-based sociologist Hakan Yavuz has expressed concern that the Hizmet Movement has become so influential in Turkey that democratic pluralism there might be harmed. Turkish debate is ripe with such concerns, which often lend themselves to conspiracy theories. It is very difficult to get a detached and nuanced assessment of the influence of Hizmet in Turkish civil society today. I, for one, am not fit to give such an assessment. What should be said is that there are hundreds of books and articles in Turkish claiming that Gülen is working to covertly Christianize Turkey, that he is an agent of the CIA, or the Vatican, that he is a Zionist and is being used by foreign interests to produce a lame and submissive version of Islam. The movement is said to have infiltrated the Turkish police force. In the US quite a few articles have been published depicting Gülen as a revolutionary Islamist. Under that mild surface he is actually planning to reinstitute the Islamic Caliphate and make Turkey into a hard line *sharia* state. He is just like Ayatollah Khomeini, they claim.

Others, like the Jesuit Thomas Michel support the movement and call it one of the major hopes for a more tolerant world. His late Catholic colleague Georges Marovitch, former ambassador for the Vatican in Turkey, has called Gülen a saint. The historian Carter Findley has suggested that Gülen and the movement around him might have a similar impact on the 21st century as Gandhi and the peace movement inspired by him had in the 20th century.[8]

---

[8]   Political scientist Doğan Koç presented a massive study of texts denouncing Gülen at an international conference at University of Chicago in November 2010. He later published his research as a book titled *Strategic Defamation of Fethullah*

What is one to think?

In the early summer of 2012 Prime Minister Recep Tayyip Erdoğan extended an invitation for Gülen to return to Turkey from the US, where he has been living since 1999. Gülen said he would not return, in part due to the state of his health, but mainly because he did not want to be made into a political tool and thus cause tension in the country. Even, when the opportunities to gain influence were ripe, Gülen insisted that his aspirations have never been political, that people should not use his message for political purposes. As noted before, Erdoğan has now decided that Gülen is the main threat to the Turkey he wants to create. We will witness how this new conflict will unfold in the near future. It should be remembered that Erdoğan is not the AK Party. The party has many other representatives, members and supporters. In the same manner Hizmet should not be too closely identified with Gülen, even if his status as its inspiration gives him a very special position.

In order to situate Gülen in a broader contemporary context, I read Gülen in light of Mohammed Bamyeh's analysis, which says that the instrumental interpretation of Islam that dominated much of the 20th century has in recent years been challenged by a more and more prominent hermeneutical movement within contemporary Islam. What Bamyeh calls an instrumental interpretation of Islam was set on using and adapting Islam for societal purposes, thus situating Islam very much in the socio-political domain and the anti- and post-colonial struggles. This interpretation of Islam was very much confined by a nation-state perspective and thus became legalistic and focused on external aspects.

The Islam of the hermeneutical movement, on the other hand, is a mode of knowledge and existence. Thereby the religion is centered on areas that by and large lie besides or beyond politics, with a personal, spiritual and more internal focus. According to Bamyeh the hermeneutical movement consists of people like Muhammad Shahrur in Syria, Abdolkarim Soroush in Iran, Mahmoud Muhammad Taha in Sudan and Fethullah Gülen in Turkey.[9]

Gülen: English vs. Turkish (University Press of America, 2012). This was also where Carter Findley compared Gülen's influence to Gandhi's.

[9] Mohammad Bamyeh, "Hermeneutics against Instrumental Reason: National and Post-National Islam in the 20th Century," *South Atlantic Quarterly* 29, no. 3 (2008).

Saba Mahmood has charted the same hermeneutical movement and analyzed it in relation to secularism. Mahmood sees the keen and supportive Western interest in the hermeneutical Muslims as driven by Imperialist-Secularist interests. She never mentions Gülen, but in her model one may arguably consider him rather a traditionalist defending orthodoxy against the hermeneutists, and thus he might be more of a nuisance to the Euro-American state perspective. The point Mahmood wants to make is that even Islamic identities that are much more orthodox and oppositional than Gülen's must be given room in a future world order, and this does not have to mean the end of liberal democracy. Democracy might take different shapes than the present version, and even if it becomes more conservative it does not necessarily mean it is less democratic. Islam does not have to become modern or hermeneutical to be acceptable.[10] Gülen would agree, even if his vocabulary and perspective is quite different from Mahmood's.

Bamyeh's and Mahmood's analysis places Gülen in a field demarcated by hermeneutical, individualized religion, modernistic secularism and a still quite unchartered global post-secular societal order. The concept of post-secularity is a vehicle for a large number of very interesting contemporary discussions around the relationships and interplay between institutionalized religion, state and individual religiosity. The different interpretations of Gülen follow major dividing lines in contemporary politics—whether democracy is an exclusive product of the Western, modern liberal order, or if democracy can also be built on Islamic sources and practices.

My aim is to give as nuanced and detailed a reflection on Gülen's writings as possible, from a post-secular perspective. In the end I do this to find my own stance on these questions. I hope that this will give the reader a richer understanding of Islam today, and thereby also give food for thought about the possible role of Turkey in the European Union, and of Islam in Europe, Sweden and the world to come, even if these are huge and possibly ungraspable questions. I also hope to foster thinking about what we—regardless of whether we are Muslims or not—might learn from a Muslim thinker like Fethullah Gülen.

---

[10]   Saba Mahmood, "Secularism, Hermeneutics and Empire: The Politics of Islamic Reformation," *Public Culture* 18, no. 2 (2006).

Chapter 2

Are You a Muslim, or What?

O ften when I talk about Islam—in private conversations or in lectures—I get the question: "Are you a Muslim, or what?" I always have difficulties answering, in the same way that I find it difficult to give a good answer to the question whether I am a Christian or not.

Can one answer "a little," or "sometimes"?

I am neither a practicing Christian, Jew nor Muslim, but to give a negative answer to the question if I am a Muslim or Christian feels like I am distancing myself from religion, as if I didn't want to have anything to do with the faith traditions. But I do want to have something to do with them. I see them as bearers of great wisdom and insight, at the same time as they have stood for, and been used to legitimate, great and systematic oppression.

For over 20 years I have been studying Islam, with the Turkish environment as my portal. I have read, discussed, traveled, lectured, written academic articles, and visited international conferences. But in some respects there have been two different tracks in my Islamic learning: one personal and existentially explorative, and one more distanced, traditionally academic. It isn't easy to let them meet in academic writing or teaching.

For a long period I limited myself to writing and speaking about prejudices about Islam in the Western Christian tradition. I thought the world had seen enough of European male academics who want to explain what Islam *is*. Often they have done it with great and sincere benevolence, but the result has still been that Muslims themselves haven't been heard. A great part of my time at the university has been spent critically investigating Orientalist conceptions of Islam and the Muslim world.

At last I have come to a point where I want, and think I should try, to speak about Islam itself, even if not in the role of a distanced academic observer. There are many introductions to Islam written from a distance—good ones, better than I could ever write. What I find missing are empathetic dialogues on what we can learn from discussing Islam, rather than what we should learn about Muslims in order to understand why they behave as they do. Thus I want to avoid the traditional, objective reporting of educational material. Instead I want to show what I have found that is alluring, inviting, stimulating, confusing and challenging—and thus show that we all, no matter who "we" are, can be enriched and can learn from joining company with the Islamic tradition.

Fethullah Gülen makes a distinction between education and learning. He holds that a school never can manage to create good, engaged, well-adjusted and God-loving persons if it is not engaged in true education. In any school, and from any teacher, students can get a lot of knowledge. But such learning can never form a person. To do that you need real education, Gülen says. This is the core of his pedagogical thinking. Every student needs and is entitled to a dedicated teacher who sees them and cares about them, who educates their whole being and does not only give them subject knowledge.[11]

Of course you could change the wording, and call the subject-orientated teaching "education" and the insightful, mentoring type of teaching "learning." It does not matter. The important thing is the distinction, and the emphasis that knowledge actually does not have an ultimate value in and of itself. Knowledge is of value if it can lead to insights, empathy and new life patterns.

There is, according to me, an overemphasis in Swedish schools on the idea that knowledge can solve conflicts and prejudice. Knowledge that does not produce insights makes no difference. You can know all that there is to know about a certain subject without having greater

---

[11] The distinction between education and learning is described in "Education from the Cradle to the Grave," *Advocate of Dialogue*, (Fairfax Virginia: The Fountain 2000).

insight into it than those without much knowledge.[12] How many facts you know about Islam doesn't say anything about your stance on the role of Islam in Swedish or Turkish society. In the Swedish parliament, populist right wing member Kent Ekeroth of the Sweden democrats, whose aim it is to stop the Islamization of Sweden, probably knows more about Islam than most other parliamentarians. His sole use of this knowledge is to insinuate that Islam is a threat to Swedish values and Swedish society.

Too much of the available scholarly literature on Islam is focused on knowledge and facts. I would rather, or in addition, try to show the insights I have gained from my studies of Islam. One might wonder if it is possible to convey insights. It is hard, and carries other dimensions than didactic learning. Even if understanding always takes place in each individual, knowledge is more connected to a methodic exposition. Insights are born in vaguer ways and include some kind of existential openness. Maybe they come more easily from a personal role model, as Gülen stresses.

I cannot claim to deliver insights. But I will keep the distinction in mind, and I will not hide behind a supposedly objective transmission of knowledge. Knowing more about each other might be a step on the road to solidarity and understanding, but a more lasting engagement is connected to insight, and probably also to a sense of humbleness, knowing that we are all, more or less, lost in the maelstrom of everyday life.

---

[12] See Ludwig Wittgenstein's discussion on knowledge and insight in *Philosophical Investigations* (1953); see for example § 209.

Chapter 3

Knowledge, Reflection, Insight

Knowledge is central in Islam. The Arabic root verb *alima* (to know) and its derived forms occur around 750 times in the Qur'an, making it one of the most frequent words, after *Allah*, *Rabb*, and the roots *k-w-n* (to be) and *q-w-l* (to say). The Qur'an states that knowledge will lead to faith, and that those who come to faith will also have knowledge (Qur'an 2:26, 30:56, 58:1).[13] According to *Sunan ibn Majah*, Prophet Muhammad said that "The search for knowledge is incumbent upon every Muslim."[14]

> The Qur'an contains many verses, such as: "Say: '*Are they equal—those who know and those who don't know?*'" (39:9), that emphasize the importance of knowledge and learning. It also warns that "*among his servants, only those who have knowledge truly fear God*" (35:28), meaning that true piety and worship is possible only through knowledge.[15]

This Qur'anic understanding of a correspondence and continuity between knowledge and faith, forwarded also by Gülen, stands in stark opposition to a modern antagonistic understanding of the relation between knowledge and faith. Western Enlightenment meant to break

---

[13] The standard work on the ideas of knowledge in classical Islam is *Rosenthal, Franz, Knowledge Triumphant: The Concept of Knowledge in Medieval Islam* (Leiden: E. J. Brill, *1970).*

[14] From Sunan ibn Majah; I quote it from William C. Chittick, *The Sufi Path of Knowledge: Ibn al-'Arabi's Metaphysics of Imagination,* (Albany: SUNY Press, 1989) 147.

[15] M. Fethullah Gülen *The Messenger of God Muhammad: An Analysis of the Prophet's Life,* (New Jersey: The Light, 2006) 194.

away from the bonds of faith and tradition and enter the realm of knowledge and reason. "*Credo quia absurdum,*" attributed to the church father Tertullian as a statement of trust in the manifest truth of the Messiah, became a slogan with a negative connotation, saying that religion equals irrationalism. A good life and a prosperous society, according to a dominant strand of the Enlightenment tradition, could be reached by replacing faith and irrationalism with objective facts and positive knowledge.[16]

Another Western tradition, closely related to Christianity, discusses knowledge in relation to wisdom. In this dichotomy knowledge has sometimes been seen as a hindrance for wisdom, as being too caught up in the material world. In the words of T. S. Elliott:

> Knowledge of words, and ignorance of The Word.
> All our knowledge brings us nearer to our ignorance,
> [...] Where is the wisdom we have lost in knowledge?[17]

This is a dichotomy that seems not to be present to the same degree in Islam as it is in other traditions, perhaps because of the recurrent reminder that man should respect the limitations of his mind.

According to the *Encylopaedia of Islam*, *ilm* is the Arabic-Islamic word for "knowledge." Related Arabic terms are *ma'rifa* (knowledge), *fiqh* (understanding), *hikma* (wisdom) and *shu'ur* (perception). Very early on in Islamic history, "*Ma'rifa* [came to mean] secular knowledge and *ilm* ... the knowledge of God, hence of anything which concerns religion," says the *Encyclopedia*. But later *ma'rifa* became a Sufi term for the spiritual knowledge of God, and *ilm* a general term for knowledge.[18] Al-Ghazali stated that "the knowledge of God (*ma'rifa*) is the end of every cognition and the fruit of every science (*ilm*) according to all schools of thought."[19]

---

[16] Max Weber "World Rejection and Theodicy," in *From Max Weber: essays in sociology.* Eds. H.H. Gerth and C.W. Mills (London: Taylor & Francis.1998[1920]) 352

[17] T. S. Eliot, *The Rock* (London: Faber & Faber, 1934).

[18] Bernard Lewis et al. "'Ilm" in *Encyclopaedia of Islam.* vol 3. (Leiden: E. J. Brill,1971) 1133

[19] Franz Rosenthal, *Knowledge Triumphant: The Concept of Knowledge in Medieval Islam.* (Leiden: E. J. Brill, 1970) 142.

How does Gülen's understanding of knowledge relate to all this? To be able to discuss this I will start with a close reading of Gülen's presentation of the central epistemological concepts in *Emerald Hills of the Heart.*

Knowledge according to Fethullah Gülen

The English rendering of Fethullah Gülen's *Emerald Hills of the Heart* presents the following definitions of the central epistemological terms:

> *'Ilm* (knowledge) means information obtained through the human senses or through Revelations or inspiration of God. It is also used to denote information that is in agreement with facts or realities, and to denote understanding something with its real, whole meaning and content."[20]

> *Ma'rifa* is the special knowledge that is acquired through reflection, sincere endeavor, using one's conscience and inquiring into one's inner world. It is different from (scientific) knowledge (*'ilm*) [...] The opposite of (scientific) knowledge is ignorance, while the opposite of *ma'rifa* is denial.[21]

> *Hikma* (wisdom) [...] has been interpreted by the exacting scholars of truth [*hakikat ulemâsı*] as being able to combine useful knowledge and righteous deeds in life. Righteous deeds are the willed outcome of knowledge applied, and the beginning of new Divine gifts.[22]

As can be deduced from these short definitions, Gülen sees both a kind of hierarchy and a complementarity between different aspects of knowledge. He also argues that knowledge has no aim in itself. Knowledge must not be reduced to an instrument for worldly gains, but it should not be restricted to learning only about religious traditions either.

> Confining knowledge to religious sciences devoid of reflection and investigation inevitably results in contentment with animal breed-

---

[20] Gülen, *Emerald Hills*, vol. 2, 18.
[21] Gülen, *Emerald Hills*, vol. 2, 135.
[22] Gülen, *Emerald Hills*, vol. 2, 26.

ing and agriculture, in idleness and the neglect of striving in the way of God. The ultimate result is misery, poverty, and humiliation.[23]

Knowledge is but the first step on the way towards a true love of God. There is "a way of light extending from belief to knowledge of God and therefrom to love of God; and then to progress to the Hereafter and God's pleasure and approval—this is the way to become a perfect, universal human being."[24] Gülen describes a link between real knowledge, true faith and right conduct. If you truly know, you will act accordingly. This is very similar to the Socratic understanding of conformity between correct knowledge and right conduct. If you behave unethically, it is because you don't have proper knowledge. This is why education is essential for a good life. Virtue is the result of good education, and good education must lead the students to "wholeness of thought and contemplation."[25]

To find this way, the tool of reflection (*tafakkur*) is central, as can be seen in the Qur'anic invocation "*Signs for a people who reflect*" (Qur'an 10:24, 13:3, 16:12, 16:69, 30:21, 39:42). In Gülen's presentation knowledge can be described as a foundation for reflection. Without proper reflection knowledge can lead also to degrading results.

> *Tafakkur* literally means to think on a subject deeply, systematically, and in great detail. In this context, it signifies reflection, which is the heart's lamp, the soul's food, the spirit of knowledge, and the essence and light of the Islamic way of life. Reflection is the light in the heart that allows the believer to discern what is good and evil, beneficial and harmful, beautiful and ugly. Again, it is through reflection that the universe becomes a book to study, and the verses of the Qur'an disclose their deeper meanings and secrets more clearly. Without reflection, the heart is darkened, the spirit is exasperated, and Islam is lived at such a superficial level that it is devoid of meaning and profundity.[26]

---

[23] Gülen, *Muhammad*, 194.
[24] Gülen, *Emerald Hills*, vol 1, 11.
[25] M. Fethullah Gülen, *Advocate of Dialogue,* compiled by Ali Ünal and Alphonse Williams, (Fairfax VA: The Fountain, 2000) 312.
[26] Gülen, *Emerald Hills*, vol 1, 10.

As I have stated, this emphasis on reflection is in tune with a growing trend in epistemology and science studies influenced by Wittgenstein and others who are more interested in the use and effects of knowledge than the classically preferred focus on the procedural aspects of knowing.

'Ilm is broadly presented as meaning simply knowledge. But the concept of knowledge presented by Gülen under the heading *'ilm* differs from what one would find in Western encyclopedias. It is important to note that the broad presentation is not central to Gülen's aim in the book. He thinks it can be useful, though, "to mention some secondary matters, such as the different types of knowledge and its sources."

The first part of the article *"Ilm* (knowledge)" in *Emerald Hills of the Heart* deals with these "secondary matters," and presents a rather scholastic exposé of the different ways knowledge can be defined. Gülen shows here that he masters the Islamic tradition and its definitions, as well as the terminology and concepts of modern science.

Gülen states that according to Islam there are three sources of knowledge: the external senses, true reports, and reason. Another way to understand knowledge is to divide it into 1) knowledge acquired through the mental faculties, and 2) reported knowledge.

Acquired knowledge 1) can be divided into:

a) Knowledge of necessary matters, such as health and education,

b) Knowledge that is disapproved of, such as sorcery, divination and occult sciences, and

c) Social and natural sciences, which Islam regards as obligatory for a good society and a good life.

It is notable that Gülen sees sorcery and occultism as knowledge, although of a disapproved kind.

Reported knowledge 2) comes in two kinds:

a) Knowledge based on spiritual discovery, and

b) Knowledge concerning Islam and Islamic life.

2a) can be either knowledge that occurs in one's heart as a gift from God, or knowledge that arise in the conscience, and

2b) can be divided into four categories:

i)   Knowledge of Islamic fundamentals, the sources of *sharia*,

ii) Knowledge of the subdivisions of *sharia*: worship, civil law, criminal law,

iii) Primary Islamic sciences: language, grammar, meaning, composition, and eloquence, and

iv) Complementary Islamic sciences: phonetics, recitation, interpretation, and exegesis.

After this thorough classification Gülen says that *Emerald Hills of the Heart* is a study of reported knowledge (of the type 2a).

As I understand it, Gülen presents his Sufi concepts as means to deepen this kind of knowledge (*'ilm* 2a) and transform it into *ma'rifa*, being the "substance of knowledge attained through reflection, intuition, and inner perception." *Ma'rifa* is "the station where knowing is united with the one who knows." The next vital point is that in order to have *ma'rifa*, "one should also have enough willpower to apply what one knows."[27] Knowledge must be transformative to be valuable. To become wisdom (*hikma*), knowledge must be combined with action. The activist aspect of Gülen's work is thus linked to the more introverted Sufi reflections, and the conception of life as service (*hizmet*), so important for the broader movement, can be deduced also from this angle. Gülen has a consistent philosophy of knowledge, education and social activism.

In discussing wisdom (*hikma*), Gülen lies close to the Aristotelian concept of *phronesis*, talking about "wisdom as correct judgment, and acting as one should act and doing what is necessary to do at the right time and the right place."[28] *Phronesis* is the ability to apply what one knows in specific circumstances, to see what is right and wrong directly as a result of experience and reflection, rather than from a rational analysis of the present situation. Again we can see a parallel in contemporary philosophy, where Aristotelian ethics have found new interest, with the concept of *phronesis* (practical reason, judgment, wisdom) as a central point.[29]

---

[27] Gülen, *Emerald Hills*, vol 2, 135, 146.

[28] Ibid., 27.

[29] Joseph Dunne, *Back to The Rough Ground: Phronesis and Techne in Modern Philosophy and in Aristotle* (Notre Dame: University of Notre Dame Press, 1998).

But acting correctly in every situation is not the final outcome of wisdom. Knowledge and wisdom are elements of the heart (*qalb*), and of the spirit (*ruh*), that is: "an individual's real nature,"[30] "the essence of human existence and nature."[31]

Has Gülen read Plato and Aristotle? Most probably he has, but still his arguments are not built on Athenian ground. Even if we can find parallels between Gülen and Western philosophical thinking this does not necessarily imply influence in any direction. Another connection can of course be traced through the importance of Plato (Aflatun) and Aristotle (Aristutalis) in the Islamic history of ideas. Especially in *Emerald Hills of the Heart*, Gülen is a clear representative of the theological school *ahl al-sunna wa'l-jama'a* (the people of tradition, example and consensus) and thus builds his arguments exclusively on Islamic sources.

The main competing theological school is often said to be theological rationalism. Saying that Gülen is more traditionalist than rationalist means that he, as has already become visible, does not fully trust reason. He is more ready to trust the example of the first generations of Muslims than rational deductions, and he seldom cites pure philosophical sources. This also means that Gülen does not stress the influence of Greek philosophy in the formation of Islamic orthodoxy. But like the rationalists Gülen stresses that God and His Creation can be understood through the reason that God has given us. Stronger rationalists, like those in the *Mutazilite* school in the Abbasid period could speak as if God and Creation were subdued to logical necessities and support conclusions such as that bodily resurrection is impossible, even if this seems to contradict the Qur'anic revelation. Gülen would never argue like that.

Tradition, interpretation, imitation

Gülen is a traditionalist; he holds that we can learn love, peace and tolerance from the example of the Prophet and the early Muslims. Literalists, fundamentalists and militant Islamists are the ones going against

---

[30] Gülen, *Emerald Hills*, vol 1, 24.
[31] Gülen, *Emerald Hills*, vol 3, 154.

tradition (*they* are modern), even if Gülen do not want to talk about modern or moderate Islam. That is not his path; he preaches a sound, broad, truly traditional Islam. An important strand in tradition is the constant re-interpretation of the examples (*Sunna*) of Prophet Muhammad to constantly understand new challenges and questions. Another important aspect of tradition is the insight that our positions will always be taken in relation to our own very limited horizons. The traditional way of ending an argument on what would be the most appropriate Islamic point of view in a specific case is to say "and God always knows best"—i. e. "I may be wrong." The self-assured arrogance shown by many militant Islamists is a modern phenomenon, influenced by Western modernity's belief in positive knowledge and objective answers. Surprisingly, many of these assured and always condemning militants have a modern scientific education rather than a traditional religious schooling.

As a traditionalist, Gülen never speaks about himself as a reformer or an innovator. He wants to reinstall Islam as a living part of the future, and holds that many of the economic, political and social problems in Muslim countries are due to losing contact with tradition.

An all too common way of portraying an Islamic history of ideas is to focus on the concepts of *taqlid* (imitation) and *ijtihad* (effort, interpretation). Especially in Western scholarship it became very common to stress that "the gates of ijtihad" (the possibility of interpretation) were closed sometime in the 10th century, and to interpret this as a first sign of the stagnation of the Islamic tradition. It is correct that some scholars in this period started to argue that there now existed a coherent and full Islamic teaching. The task from now on was to follow this path. Maybe more importantly, firmer guidelines and frames were developed around what one should know in order to be counted as a legitimate and trustworthy interpreter (*mujtahid*) of tradition. Most Islamic scholars still talked about the constant need of interpretation at the same time as they saw that only the most educated had the skills and the knowledge to engage in *ijtihad*. There was also a great concern against engaging in innovative interpretation. Innovation (*bid'ah*) denotes all practices or beliefs that do not find support in the example of the Prophet. Maybe it is more correct to say that the danger of *bid'ah* strongly restricted the space for interpretation, rather than to talk about the closing of the gates of *ijtihad*. Only a very limited number of scholars thought that interpretation had come to an end.[32]

To understand the relations between *taqlid—ijtihad—bid'ah* better, more conceptual clarifications are necessary. This means even more Arabic terms. I think this is unavoidable in order to see the complexities in how tradition and interpretation have been lived. The first generation of modern reformist Muslim thinkers in the late 19th century—men like al-Thatawi, Khayr al-Din, Muhammad Abduh and Sayyid Ahmad Khan—pointed to the distinction between that which concerns the relation between God and men (*ibadat*), and that which concerns relations among men (*mu'amalat*). On *ibadat*, concerning Prayer, worship and the fundaments of faith, we find detailed and eternal guidelines in the Qur'an and *Sunna*. Here there is no room for other than imitation (*taqlid*). But in social issues (*mu'amalat*) the sources gives only general directions tied to the specific social, political and economic circumstances of that time in history. The distinction between *ibadat* and *mu'amalat* is also stressed by Tariq Ramadan as a means to acknowledge the importance of both *taqlid* and *ijtihad* in Islam, and thus to mediate between those stuck in a modernistic either-or.[33]

As will be made clearer later on, Gülen had a traditional schooling that was quite un-influenced by this reform movement. Gülen formulates his positions from a broad understanding of traditional Islam. This is the reason why the opposition between *ijtihad* and *taqlid,* so important for Western Islamology, does not seem very interesting to him. He rather represents the traditional view that those who do not have deep

---

[32] Wael B. Hallaq, "Was the Gate of Ijtihad Closed?" *International Journal of Middle East Studies* 16 vol. 1, (1984). A very good brief introduction to classical Islamic theology, in my opinion, is Binyamin Abrahamov, *Islamic theology: Traditionalism and Rationalism* (Edinburgh: Edinburgh University Press, 1998).

[33] Tariq Ramadan, *Radical Reform: Islamic Ethics and Liberation* (Oxford: Oxford University Press, 2009). On the first generation of Islamic modernists: Albert Hourani, *Arabic Thought in the Liberal Age 1798–1939* (Cambridge: Cambridge University Press, 1983).

knowledge of the Qur'an, *Sunna*, the Arabic language, and the theological traditions will have no option but to follow the tradition (*taqlid*), while those working within the tradition always needs to make new efforts (*ijtihad*) to be able to interpret its content in light of their own times and the specific problems and possibilities facing them. But Gülen never says that he has conducted *ijtihad*, or that he is a *mujtahid*. Instead he holds, as do many contemporary Islamic scholars, that it is no longer possible to see a *mujtahid* as one individual. The type of Renaissance man with thorough knowledge of every scientific and social field *mujtahid* would require is simply not feasible in today's specialized world. This is why works of interpretation should be conducted by *ijtihad* committees, where people from a variety of scientific and religious fields of specialization work together.

It can also be noted that Gülen does not work within the field of Islamic jurisprudence (*fiqh*). And strictly speaking *ijtihad* is a *fiqh* method that is to be used when the methods of analogy (*qiyas*) and consensus (*ijma*) cannot give an answer to a specific problem or question. A *fiqh* scholar that can give an answer (*fatwa*) on the basis of *ijtihad* is a *mujtahid*. Gülen does not give *fatwas*, he formulates his answers not from inventories of the different positions taken within *fiqh*, but rather by way of freer advice given in conversations (*sohbet*).

From a sociological point of view Gülen is a modern Muslim, acting in networks and through informal and digital channels, rather than from traditional positions or centers of learning. In this way he is a part of what Dale Eickelman and others have called a growing new public sphere in the Muslim world.[34] It is important, though, not to see the public sphere as something monolithic, that everywhere it must have the same shape and function as it has gotten in the European tradition, as has been a norm in much the dominant theories of democracy. One of my interests is to understand better what importance and influence Turkish Islam has and might have in the possible formation of what more and more people talk about as a post-secular global public sphere tran-

---

[34] Dale Eickelman & Jon W. Anderson (red.), *New Media in the Muslim World: The Emerging Public Sphere* (Bloomington: Indiana University Press, 2003).

scending the alleged opposition between secularism and Islam (or religion as such).

Gülen might be said to be theologically traditional and sociologically modern, even if this is still too simplified. Like many pairs of concepts taken for granted, the dichotomies of public-private, traditional-modern and *taqlid-ijtihad* are too blunt when it comes to describing concrete phenomena. Gökhan Bacık has called Gülen "amodern;" a position that does not accept the dichotomy that the concepts *traditional-modern* tries to make us believe in.[35]

Gülen claims that interpretation (*ijtihad*) is necessary for the survival of religion; one of the goals of education is to give people the tools to become *mujtahid*s. Interpretation must rest on deep knowledge; if a crude focus on current necessity (*darura*) and the common good (*maslaha*) had guided interpretation through history there would be nothing left of Islam, Gülen says.

> Time and conditions are important means to interpret the Qur'an. The Qur'an is like a rose that develops a new petal every passing day and continues to blossom. In order to discover its depths and obtain its jewels in these deeper layers, a new interpretation should be made at least every 25 years.[36]

İhsan Yılmaz describes Gülen's method as *"ijtihad* through conduct," and Özcan Keleş stresses that what he is doing is "incremental *ijtihad,*" which means that his reinterpretations are developed in small and careful steps; only after a number of displacing statements does he reach a new conclusion.[37] This can be observed in his gradual denial of the punishment for apostasy, for example. During the 1970s Gülen was engaged in "incremental *ijtihad,*" moving on to state openly in the 1990s

---

[35] Gökhan Bacık presented at the aforementioned conference in Chicago.

[36] Gülen, *Advocate of Dialogue*, 52.

[37] İhsan Yılmaz, "*Ijtihad* and *Tajdid* by Conduct: The Gülen Movement" in *Turkish Islam and the Secular State: The Gülen Movement*, ed. John L Esposito and Hakan Yavuz, (Syracuse: Syracuse University Press, 2003). Özcan Keleş, "Promoting Human Rights Values in the Muslim World: The Case of the Gülen Movement" in İhsan Yılmaz (ed.) *Muslim World in Transition: Contributions of the Gülen Movement*, (London: Leeds University Press, 2007).

that what the relevant sources are talking about is not really abandoning one's faith, but desertion in war. In today's peaceful societies it does not mean the same thing to change one's religion as it did then, and the punishment meted out by tradition should only concern outright desertion, something which is also punishable in most modern states. The eventual punishment accruing to the one who abandons his faith will be given on the last day, the Day of Judgment. And, as we know, the Lord moves in mysterious ways, and we should not try to take His justice in our own hands.

If we start by stressing the central role of reflection, the opposition between *taqlid* (imitation) and *ijtihad* (interpretation) becomes somewhat odd. Is it even possible to imagine a reflecting imitation? At the same time it is obvious that reflection will make us humble towards the limits of our reason, and thus conscious of the responsibility coming with every labor of interpretation. What interests are guiding my interpretations? How honest am I? And have I really respectfully listened to all the other possible interpretations presented within tradition? What right do I have to say that this is the best, most plausible interpretation? These questions should remind us that writing a book which tries to present insights is somewhat self-righteous, and most probably portrays the author as cleverer and more relaxed than he can really be.

The traditional Western field of epistemology is not very interested in the kinds of knowledge discussed by Gülen in *Emerald Hills of the Heart*. It is hard to find a definition of knowledge allowing knowledge that appears in one's heart to be called knowledge. According to the Sufis, knowledge is "the light and radiation that come from the realms beyond the material world and have their source in God's knowledge," and as such it is outside of modern epistemology.[38] It might seem hard to find openings for a real dialogue about the concept of knowledge in Islam (as expressed in Gülen's thought) and in Western philosophy (generally). They are at best incommensurable; at worst Western philosophy negates Sufi knowledge as meaningless.

---

[38]   Gülen, *Emerald Hills,* vol 2, 23.

Gülen writes that knowledge also covers the meaning of the modern scientific term instinct, what Gülen calls innate knowledge and categorizes as "knowledge without means." This shows that the Islamic conception of knowledge is broader than the *episteme*-centered Western concept. I will return to Gülen's conception of knowledge later, when I discuss his relation to science.

Reconnection

It took quite some time before I came in contact with the Hizmet Movement again after that afternoon in Afyon. The interest in Islam that had been awoken in Turkey made me want to visit other Muslim countries. The winter previous to the Afyon incident I had worked in Egypt and Israel. The following winter took me to Morocco. From very early on I felt that much of what I read about Islam was too focused on the Arab world. I wanted to experience how Islam was lived and practiced in other major Muslim countries. During 1994 and 1995 I worked in Indonesia, the world's largest Muslim country. It became more and more clear to me that Islam did not necessarily look like the examples from the Arab world given in most of the books I came across. To me, it rather seemed that the most interesting and vital discussions went on in other locations, for example in Turkey and Indonesia.

I was becoming increasingly aware that I could not live in a suitcase traveling around with tour groups forever. It was a lonely life, and it wasn't very healthy to spend the evenings in various hotel bars. I moved back to Sweden, to Gothenburg on the West coast, to study and try to satisfy my curiosity along an academic road.

Sometime during the autumn semester of 1997, as I was working on Middle Eastern studies and the history of (Western) philosophy, I had a request from a small Swedish magazine to contribute an article on Islam with a thematic focus on God. This was my first ever request to be in a proper publication, something I had striven for but hadn't known how to achieve. I wrote a piece about the role of Islam in contemporary Turkey and Indonesia, but in the end the editors thought my piece didn't really fit in with the other texts. I was piling on facts in

the text; in hindsight also I can see this. Still, my research for the article gave me renewed contact with the Gülen Movement. Among other
things I wrote about how Sufism had come to be a part of new age
spirituality, which also has a broad following in Turkey's secular middle classes.

From the article:

> In more organized form the new age tendencies can be seen in the
> Nakşibendi related Nur-movement, estimated to have at least one
> million followers. Its leader is Fethullah Gülen Hodjaefendi—an influ-
> ential preacher who puts more weight on the inner experience of
> God than on the formal law. The movement runs and finances many
> schools where science is highly praised as a means to better under-
> stand Creation and its wonders. It also runs a TV-channel called
> *Samanyolu*, the 'Milky Way.' The members of Nur are mostly found
> in the bigger cities of Western Turkey, where modernity is most
> developed.

I did not know much more than this, and most of it came from a
leaflet from the Swedish Institute of International Affairs on Islam and
politics in Turkey, by Elisabeth Özdalga.[39] One can see that I interpreted the movement as some kind of new age spirituality. I think it was
the name of the TV-channel—the Milky Way—that made me think about
astrology, and this combined with a leader focusing on experience rather than law led me to imagine a figure quite unlike the real Mr. Gülen.
It is also outright incorrect to say that Gülen holds experience higher
than the law. It was probably just as well that this article never made
it into print. Then again, I will most probably be just as critical of what
I write now ten years on. That's life.

---

[39]   Elisabeth Özdalga, *Islam i turkisk politik*, Världspolitikens dagsfrågor nr 2, 1996.

Chapter 4

Fethullah Gülen and Turkish Islam

The main character in this book is Fethullah Gülen. I want to stress this. I am not a sociologist, and I do not claim to know all the workings and influences of the movement inspired by Fethullah Gülen. I am a reader of texts, and I have spent a lot of time reading Mr. Gülen's texts. I have also spent a lot of time in Turkey, and I will try to place Gülen's texts in this Turkish context. One could say that Gülen is the broker between me and the Islamic tradition. At least this is how I have plotted this book. It can thus be read as an introduction to Gülen, even if the title is chosen to show that the scope is both more personal and broader than a classical introductory textbook.

Next to Gülen (and me), Bediüzzaman Said Nursi is the person that will be given most attention. He lived a generation before Gülen and is his most important predecessor.

I take my examples from Gülen and Said Nursi, examples that should also give a broader picture of contemporary Islam, Turkey and of a possible relationship to the Islamic tradition.

By profession I am a historian of Ideas, trained to read philosophical texts, to answer historical questions and discuss broader problems via texts. As said, this is also what I am doing in this book, even if it is not a regular research report. It is a book where I reflect on contemporary Islam, mostly on the basis of texts, but also in relation to personal encounters with people who in different ways are inspired by these texts.

According to the records of the Turkish bureaucracy, Muhammed Fethullah Gülen was born on the 27th of April 1941, in a village named

Korucuk in the Pasinler district of Erzurum province in northeastern Anatolia. In the preface to many of his books it says:

> Fethullah Gülen, "Hocaefendi" (pronounced "Hodja effendi") in the words of those who respect and love him, was born in the village of Korucuk, Pasinler, Erzurum in Turkey, in 1938. Due to the slow pace of life in villages, he was registered later in the official ledger. For this reason, the official entry in the ledger states 27th of April 1941.

It is not unknown that in the remoter provinces of Turkey the registration of births with the authorities was not of high priority. Gülen started primary school in 1946 and eventually got his license as an imam in 1959. This points to 1938 as a more probable year of birth.

What is more interesting than his exact time of birth is that, as Fethullah moved with his family to the village of Alvar, he quit school after only three years—he only had three years of formal education. From then on he had no public education. He helped in the household and herded the family's cows and sheep. In addition to these daily chores he was trained in reading the Qur'an by his mother and in the Arabic language by his father, who was an imam. Gülen states that he started praying the regulated Prayers (namaz) at the age of four, and that he hasn't missed a Prayer since.

Later his education continued with other religious scholars in Erzurum's traditional religious madrasa educational system, which was still quite well functioning. He came under the schooling of Said Effendi, grandson to the great local Sufi master Alvarlı Muhammed Lütfi. Gülen often speak about Lütfi as one of the grand Turkish thinkers, paired with more well-known names like Mawlana Jalaluddin Rumi and Yunus Emre. Political scientist Gökhan Bacık has stressed that this "amodern" educational milieu that formed Gülen is important in order to understand his thinking, not least in comparison to other, more modernist contemporary Islamic intellectuals. The scholars (ulama) that trained Gülen had no modern connection to the state, they had no idea about influencing a state, instead they acted in the sphere of daily life without connections to nationalism or modernity, Bacık claims. This might be one explanation why Gülen is not attracted to new and modern ideas about an Islamic state, or an Islamic legal system.[40] It is really only in the 20th century, in the radical Muslim discussions on the role of *sharia* in a modern context, that an idea of an Islamic state based solely on *sharia* was developed, by thinkers like Mawlana Mawdudi in Pakistan and Sayyid Qutb in Egypt. This is also the time when the thought of re-establishing the Islamic caliphate as a means to establish one state for all Muslim lands was developed, formulated by al-Nabahani in Palestine in the 1950s. It is an idea of the caliphate that has little to do with the historical caliphate which always combined the scholarly interpretations of *sharia* with local traditional law (*örf*) and civil law (*kanun*).[41] In line with the traditional view Gülen does not see *sharia* as a collection of laws, but as a source of guidance covering all aspects of a life lived in accordance with the will of God.

Scott Siraj al-Haqq Kugle recounts a parable to explain *sharia*: One of the original meanings of the word in Arabic denoted a path like the ones formed by an unruly flock of sheep as it is lead to the well by its good shepherd. This is not a narrow path but a wide string of pathways, single tracks intersecting, merging and departing as the sheep are gently driven towards the same end. The sheep take the road nature allows; sometimes they must swerve for a rock, most of them might take one turn, some are taken a bit astray and find another path ahead, and the most adventurous will make their way through unchartered land. The shepherd leads them to such extent that he makes sure that they all reach the same end, but he doesn't take much notice of the exact track each of them choose, and he sees the futility in trying to make them all walk on a straight line.[42] This is the way traditional *sharia* functions; it has always allowed for differences and diversity within the framework of a common source. The Islamic modernists who seek to emphasize *sharia* as an alternative to a state law have left tradition. Any historic state

---

[40] Gökhan Bacık presented at the mentioned conference in Chicago.

[41] On the caliphate and on law in David Waines, *An introduction to Islam*, (Cambridge: Cambridge University Press, 2003), p. 99 and p. 243.

[42] Scott Siraj al-Haqq Kugle, *Homosexuality in Islam: Critical reflections on gay, lesbian, and transgender muslims*, (Oxford: Oneworld Publications, 2010)132–133.

that has seen itself as Islamic has also had a secular law (*kanun*) as a complement for all the issues where *sharia* gives no guidance.

If Gülen can be said to be anyone's disciple, it is Lütfi's. It was in Lütfi and his grandson that Gülen had living examples. All that additionally shaped his views is a result of his readings. And Gülen is a reader of great proportions. He may lack formal education, but his learning is clearly broad and deep. The students of his I have met all testify to his almost manic studies of the Qur'an and collections of *hadith*, the great Islamic classics, as well as modern science. It is also evident in his texts that he constantly develops and deepens his thinking, in relation to its place in a changing world, but also in relationship to a wide classical Islamic canon, where Turkish and Persian works are more important than other contemporary Sunni preachers and thinkers.

The year after Lütfi's death in 1956 Gülen came in contact with the *Risale-i Nur*, the great work of the Kurdish thinker and preacher Bediüzzaman Said Nursi. Gülen was greatly influenced by Said Nursi's more modernist interpretation, and he is often considered as part of the Nur Movement, the aspect of Turkish Islam which draws its main inspiration from Said Nursi. But Gülen does not speak of Said Nursi as *üstad*, which is the usual reverential term given him by those who see him as their guide. It is probable that Gülen has never been a devoted follower of Said Nursi, and that the Gülen Movement is not really an offshoot of the Nur Movement. Gülen was very young when Said Nursi died, and the two never met. However, the *Risale-i Nur* has probably been the most important source of inspiration for Gülen, as it has been for the movement, even if it has been said that its importance has diminished somewhat in the 21st century.

Many have pointed out that one cannot understand Gülen's work and thinking if one does not know of Said Nursi's work. Perhaps we can say that Gülen has tried to pursue the course set out by Said Nursi in the *Risale-i Nur*. The work is a recurring reference in Gülen's thinking, even if the Qur'an and *Sunna* are much more frequently invoked. Even the broader classical Islamic canon takes a bigger place than Said Nursi. The most cited thinker by Gülen is Mawlana Jalaluddin Rumi. It seems that Gülen represents Said Nursi's aims and method, rather than his exact words, an approach that in my opinion is sympathetic. It will be interesting to see how Gülen's legacy will be treated by his followers once his productive days are over.

In 1959 Gülen received his license to preach from the presidency of religious affairs (*Diyanet*), and he became an imam in the northwestern city of Edirne. In 1966 he was transferred to İzmir. It was in İzmir he started to direct his attention more to education and by the end of the 1960s he had inspired so many students that it is possible to start talking about a movement. It has been growing and growing ever since.

The relations between those who follow Gülen, the people often called *Fethullahcı*'s in Turkey, who call Gülen Hodjaefendi, and those primarily following Said Nursi, who are called *Nurcu*s and call Said Nursi *üstad*, are close but also tense. As is often the case with groups close to each other there is also strong rivalry. Many of the older *Nurcus* feel that Gülen has never taken any real risks: He was not there during the early hard years when Said Nursi's followers were harassed and persecuted (even if Gülen was only a child back then). Gülen came aboard only after it was comparably safe to talk about the *Risale-i Nur*. Some older *Nurcus* see him as opportunistic and too state-friendly.

In 1990 Gülen started to publish simplified selections from the *Risale-i Nur*, which was quite difficult to read. It seemed as if Gülen was going to work his way through the 6,000 pages and explicate them in a simplified form. This effort was met with strong critique from Nur groups in Turkey who claimed that any simplification would mean that the deeper content would be lost. Gülen was forced to abandon his project.

This effort can be interpreted in two different ways. It can be seen as almost imperialistic—"I am the one who can interpret Said Nursi." But it can also be seen as a relaxed and intellectual approach to one of Islam's many important works. As with any other book, it needs to be commented on, contextualized, and explained in contemporary language. Part of the resistance against Gülen's articles shows an almost sect-like reverence for the *Risale-i Nur*, even if it is correct that an interpretation of a text can never transmit all the layers of meaning of the original text.

According to Gürkan Çelik, writer of a sociological dissertation on the Gülen Movement, it was after the critique of the *Risale-i Nur* explications that Gülen instead decided to turn to a discourse on the key concepts in the practice of Sufism, ending up with the four volume *Emerald Hills of the Heart*.

In 1999 Gülen left Turkey and went to the US for medical treatment. Due to the political persecution that erupted in the meantime he moved to the small town of Saylorburg in the Pocono Mountains of Pennsylvania, USA, and lives there since then. After ten years, he received his green card and was acknowledged as an internationally renowned scholar with a right for permanent residence in the US. It has been during Gülen's years in the US that the movement's international reach has grown.

I wonder, though, if this kind of chronological account of a person's lifespan, painted from secondary sources, can really give any insight. The idea behind this book was to avoid the role of the presumably all-knowing researcher. I think I have to restart from another beginning.

As a student I spent the second half of the 1990s focusing on Islamic subjects. I wrote essays and theses on the foreign policy cooperation between Iran and Syria, on the image of Islam and Sufism in Swedish newspapers, and on what the research literature on Islamism really meant by the concepts of fundamentalism, Islamism and Islamic resurgence.

Above all I read Edward Said, the US-Palestinian professor in comparative literature at Colombia University. He became a paragon for me. One of his most important lessons was, bluntly stated, that most of what had been written about Islam said more about the writers and their lands and times than it did about Islam and Muslims. Reading Said lead me on to his masters, French postmodern thinkers like Michel Foucault and Jacques Derrida, who made me realize that knowledge could be used to exploit, oppress and uphold power. I became very fascinated and moved by their critique of the Western tradition. It led me deep into an investigation of the darker sides of the tradition I was educated in. The result of these readings was my PhD thesis in the history of ideas, where I tried to understand how the modern Swedish self-image has affected the ways we have viewed and portrayed the outside world. My material consisted of tourism advertisements. This project can be seen as a dispute with my past as a philosophically inclined tourism worker who spent his time reading the Western classics.

After five years of PhD work I felt I had said what I had to say on the subject of tourism. I wanted to return to Turkey. In parallel with my dissertation work I had been teaching Islamic philosophy and I was now trying to find a way to combine my interests. I was also growing more and more tired of always being critical of the racism, colonialism and bigotry of my own tradition. The Swedish joke "He wanted to change the world—but he was always only opposing everything" started to feel all too real for me.

Chapter 5

Can Gülen Represent Islam?

As with all great traditions, Islam contains material for almost any kind of practice, way of life, and type of politics. And many different paths have been portrayed as legitimately Islamic—everything from non-violence and interreligious dialogue to war and ethnic cleansing. The same goes for Christianity, Hinduism and most other religions.

This means that it is quite futile to try to give an objective answer as to what is an authentic Islamic point of view, or proper Muslim conduct. We can only answer such a question if we chose to focus on a specific and limited part of tradition and adhere to a specific interpretation. This is one of the reasons why this book is focused on Fethullah Gülen's specific interpretation of Islam.

Gülen is an important thinker of global proportions. He is also in many ways a traditionalist who appears to stand for a classical and non-provocative interpretation of Islam. I would claim that the representation of Islam in this book is more representative of Islam than for example Hamas, or the current Iranian regime, or fundamentalist Wahhabism or neo-Salafism. I am aware that this is an ideological and theological claim, not a distanced empirical one.

The majority of Western representations of Islam are of the Arab world. But Islam is lived and expressed in many other regions, by many other peoples. Arabs, and the Arab world, are only a small part of the Muslim world. According to a survey from 2009, which included 232 countries of the world, 23 percent of the world's population is Muslim, which adds up to something like one and a half billion individuals. Around

50 countries have a Muslim majority population, and at most, only 20 percent of the world's Muslims can be classified as Arab. Half of the Muslims in the world live in South and Southeast Asia. The ten countries with the largest number of Muslims are: Indonesia, Pakistan, India, Bangladesh, Turkey, Egypt, Iran, Nigeria, China and Ethiopia. Nine of these ten largest Muslim countries are not Arab.[43] The Arab language is in many ways *the* Islamic language, the language of the Qur'an. But this does not mean that the Arab people, or the Arab world, have a privileged role in Islam, as Prophet Muhammad himself said (according to Ibn Hanbal): "No Arab is superior to any non-Arab; no white person is superior to any black person."[44]

It is important that the public understanding of Islam is enriched by more non-Arab examples. If we turn our eyes to large Muslim countries like Indonesia, India, Malaysia or Turkey, the image will change. There are a lot of interesting debates going on; debates that more people in the West should take note of. In this book we approach a Turkish voice.

There is a lot of talk about the need for religious and intercultural dialogue. In my understanding, religions or cultures themselves cannot dialogue. Who shall talk? If we put a copy of the Bible and the Qur'an next to each other the only result is silence. To have a dialogue, we need concrete and specific individuals interpreting their religion and culture. Thus dialogue is always between individual persons, not between traditions, cultures or religions.

As I have been saying, it is always possible to find counter arguments and oppositional examples to any point of view presented as truly Islamic, Christian, European, or whatever you like. For example, the claim that Islam is a threat to Europe is only empty demagogy to me. It depends entirely on what you understand by the denominators 'Islamic' and 'European.' If Islam is taken to be equal with Osama bin Laden's representation, and Europe to be equal to human rights and democracy it is of course true. But if we instead see Islam as equal to the fundamental

---

[43] Statistics from pewforum.org/uploadedfiles/Topics//Demographics/Muslimpopulation.pdf

[44] Sunan Ibn Hanbal 5:441.

understanding that all are equal unto God, and Europe to mean the efforts to stop refugees entering the European Union it is rather the opposite.

As Stockholm-based artist Damir Niksic has put it in his Muslim-European Nationality Proclamation:[45]

> We are not here to colonize.
> We are not here to Islamize.
> [...]
> But we are here—to stay!
> [...]
> We are the next generation of Europeans.
> Europe is our home!
> [...]
> Those who believe that we are not compatible with Europe—
> They are right in many ways.
> We do not fit that Europe, that Old Europe which insists upon backward ideologies.
> [...]
> As a matter of fact—we reject that Europe!
> We reject its racism!
> We reject its Fascism!
> We reject its Nazism!
> We reject its Orientalism,
> its Social-Orientalism!
> We reject its prejudices!
> We reject its myths!
> We reject its backwardness!
> [...]
> Our culture is Muslim-European culture.
> [...]
> We are not afraid of freedom!
> We are not afraid of responsibility!
> Our intention, our "niyyat" is pure, honest, sincere and good.
> [...]
> Once we are accepted as a European nation, not as a religious group, ethnic minority, immigrant minority and "eternal diaspora," Europe will never repeat its negative history again.
> Not on our watch!

---

[45] www.damirniksic.com

As can be seen here—the concepts Europe and Islam are so contested that they mean very little on their own. Gülen asserts that his Islamic tradition is fit to solve the problems of Europe and thus to realize the true Idea of Europe. With the help of Islam we can strengthen human rights and gain a truer democracy, he claims. He might be right, even if such broad and sweeping formulations always need to be critically discussed, which is exactly what I aim to do.

Chapter 6

Research, Objectivity, Dialogue

I do not want to present myself as an objective researcher who can say what is true and what is false. This is why I repeatedly write 'I.' It might seem self-absorbed. But it is in fact (also) the result of an epistemological claim.

Truth is nothing to be easily rejected. But in order for us to be able to refer to something as true, it must be as a result of a broad discussion. The thought that any single individual could grasp all relevant facts and experiences and put forth a summation of how things really are seems highly unlikely to me. To write and talk in a way that makes such claims should be avoided; I certainly do not want to make any such large claims. Of course I do believe strongly in the value of my interpretation, but I am also aware that it can only be my interpretation. It is limited because of all my limitations. I am not as good at Turkish as I would like to be, I haven't met as many representatives of the Hizmet Movement as I should have to know all its different interpretations, there are a lot of important books that I have never found the time to read, and I personally have a number of flaws and weaknesses.

I am for example very aware of the fact that my interpretations are dependent on the fact that I am a man, that I am heterosexual. This has had a great impact on my possibilities to meet and participate in many Turkish Muslim milieus. Even if I would like to think that I have a developed a non-gendered perspective I do not have the existential experiences of a woman or a homosexual person. I am convinced that I would be more critical had I been a woman.

In a global comparison, I think that one of the fields in which Sweden is a pioneer is on the issue of gender equality. As a Swede I am thus often critical of the gender understandings of other milieus and traditions. It is important to stress that there are still inequalities in Sweden, in relation to power, pay and freedom of lifestyle. It is also important to stress that the relative gender equality we have is mostly results of recent political struggles and decisions. Things have changed quite fast, and this means they might also change in other countries and traditions. But as was said, Sweden still has its share of patriarchal oppression, but on a different level than in Taliban-controlled Afghanistan, for example. Patriarchy is everywhere, but the differences are also major. There is a big difference between the harsh patriarchal oppression of women and gender apartheid of certain countries like Saudi Arabia, and the lack in gender equality of countries like Sweden. What I am trying to say here is that it is important for me to be a feminist, both politically and in my daily life as a husband and father. I must take full share and responsibility in the care of my children; I should know what sizes of clothes they wear, if they need new socks, to be there to comfort and see them when they need it. We have a very extensive right to paid parental leave in Sweden. This means I have been able to spend over a year at home with my children, being their primary caretaker when my wife was working. My opportunity to be a primary caretaker is the result of political priorities, and I think it affects all institutions in society if we have more men and women who have this experience and perspective. There is still a minority of Swedish families who prioritize that men take their full share as "house husbands," to use that phrase. I am convinced it makes societies better, and more prone *not* to make distinctions in private and social responsibilities because of gender. I also know that in a global context this is an odd position to hold, not the least as a man. I know Sweden has been portrayed as a totalitarian feminist-socialist state by Fox news and the likes. I also know that my ideals and practice are at odds with many Muslims positions on gender issues.

It might also be odd to have to say this: I am critical of the multiculturalist tendency to be more forgiving of a Turkish man who beats his wife than of a Swedish man who does the same. What I believe to be right and wrong, I believe to be right and wrong, irrespective of who conducts the deed. It shouldn't be strange or alarming, should it? Of course there are always circumstances that affect the possibilities different persons have when it comes to breaking patterns and established notions from their upbringing. But this can only be an explanation, and should never serve as an excuse. In this respect I see ethics as universal. But in contrast to all the European populist nationalists and other assimilationists, I am not unreflectively positive that the ethics I have been brought up with, and have come to see as mine, is the only possible one for our society. I realize that I would have thought quite differently had I been brought up somewhere else. I cannot see that there are any strict and objective criteria to deliberate in ethical questions. I thus do not believe in a divine sanction, as some others do.

This means we have to be open and reflective, we must try our very best to see the value in other ways of understanding the world, and as far as it is possible we must question and reevaluate what we have taken to be true and right. This is of course easy to say, but very hard to do. To me it is essential to read Islamic thinkers like Fethullah Gülen to get access to other paths that sometimes challenge my underlying assumptions. When something seems odd and strange it is important to try very hard to understand why. What am I really defending when I defend my position? What in me is it that is challenged by this different view? Often I can see that my own position has been too limited and self-assured. Sometimes I am convinced that the arguments for my position actually are better, that Gülen has missed something. Then I will try to convey this in a way that promotes dialectic knowledge formation and continued mutual respect. Together we can reach further and understand more, if we do not bury ourselves in opposing trenches defending our pride. We must also be forgiving towards each other if we act offensively in reaction to having a wounded pride. It will happen.

My knowledge and my experiences are limited, as are my abilities. But so are everyone else's. I still think I am able to understand and produce sound interpretations of Gülen's writings, even if readers with different experiences of Islam will inevitably see other things and possibly hold radically different opinions. I hope that you who read will be challenged to find a position of your own, and to seek out more nuanced interpretations. To invite to dialogue as much as possible I will try to hold an existential perspective alive and present. It is not only a matter of what other people think, it is also always about me—and you, and all of us. As most other people I have my hang ups, spots where I become irrational and will defend my pride and vanity rather than listen to sound arguments.

To make the dialogical ambition more precise and graspable I will think and talk about it under the name of 'border thinking.' Throughout the book the idea of border thinking will return and be developed. The mother of border thinking is Gloria Anzaldúa (1942–2004). Anzaldúa's way of mixing English and Spanish text, poetry and theoretical reflection, and autobiographical fragments in her texts has been a very important challenge and inspiration to me.[46] How can one write to best convey the fragmentary and flapping character of life and thought? Anzaldúa has a stronger confidence in the candid voice than she has in methodological stringency or theoretical distance. Her constant subject matter is life-in-between; between Mexico-Spanish and US-English; between patriarchy and poetic freedom; between rationalism and experience. She challenges all those who claim that belonging to one side of the border gives a stronger and more secure identity. On the contrary, the borderland gives us opportunities to have a fuller identity; to live life to the core. This is not only a romantic cliché. It is no bed of roses to live a lesbian lifestyle in a patriarchal environment; it is no piece of cake trying to be a writer coming from traditional surroundings where books and learning are despised. It is not easy to be seen as foreign in the US even though your family has lived in the same place for hundreds of years (Anzaldúa came from a province captured by the US from Mexico in the mid-19th century).

Still, the solution to a lack of identity can never be to force oneself into established and accepted categories. In the borderland new connections can be made, new solutions may be born. The future lies in

---

[46] Gloria Anzaldúa, *Borderlands/La Frontera: The new Mestiza*, (San Francisco: Aunt Lute Books, 1999).

intercrossing traditions, in taking ways of knowing beside the Western one seriously, and thus being able to see and grasp more. I am confident about this. Western dominance is fading, or at least is about to be re-formulated. In order for people like me, who have been born and raised in the dominant sphere, to be able to know the world differently we must make an effort to get inside the mindset of other traditions and ways of thinking—we must aspire to border thinking.

The need to transcend borders is at the same time an important aspect of the Western idea of development and progress. The father of modern philosophy René Descartes himself talked about the need to have "one foot in one land, the other foot in another country." It is a motto taken up by the German-US philosopher Fred Dallmayr. Dallmayr has written extensively on the need to think through different traditions, and has taken an interest in Muslim, Hindu and Chinese thinking, besides his own German schooling. He cites his German colleague Bernhard Waldenfels, who has worked on combining German and French thought, discussing the borders between these closely interconnected traditions. Waldenfels says that we need to plant our feet first in one country, then in another. We must take a position on one side instead of trying to hoover neutrally over both lands. In this way we can eventually find a belonging and presence on both sides of the border, and eventually reach beyond dichotomies.[47]

I am not as sure what my side of the border should be, where I ought to start in order to take that first step over the border. The difference between being schooled in a vigorous German philosophical tradition and in a broad Scandinavian context is strong. In Sweden it has never been that obvious what our intellectual tradition is. Maybe it is a German Kantian tradition, Lutheran Protestantism, or a broader and vaguer European progressive modernism, or democratic socialism, or old Swedish farm style common sense—or? My own theoretical belonging has been centered on various post-groupings.

---

[47] Quotes on Descartes and Bernhard Waldenfels from Fred Dallmayr, *Achieving Our World: Toward a Global and Plural Democracy* (Lanham: Rowman and Littlefield, 2001) 130.

The reason I bring in Waldenfels is that it is probably impossible to be a neutral reporter of other ways of thinking. A report of another way of thinking is inevitably also a report of my own way of thinking. Apart from acknowledging and seeing my own Swedish versions of the colonial and imperialistic legacies I think there might lie liberating potential in thinking deeper about what the different versions of Swedishness might mean. This goes for most national traditions and identities, but since I happen to be Swedish this is inescapably my example.

To start with, I think it is important to provincialize Sweden. For far too long Sweden has been trying to portray itself as the most modern country in the world, the most rational of all the rational. At the same time both modernity and rationalism are in many ways imported goods. I would rather focus on the skewed aspects of Swedish experience: the experience of living in a sparsely populated outskirt of the world, speaking a language that has never, ever been seen as a medium for great and important thoughts, the feeling of decenteredness coming from the fact that all great thoughts have been formulated in other languages. All these should be seen as assets, experiences that can make one connect with and feel compassion for the majority of the world's population. Provincializing one's identity is not the same thing as not being proud of one's tradition or history. It is about reinterpreting it, about identifying with the mundane and ordinary, instead of pretending to be one of the greats, commemorating victories, atrocities and great men. It is not one's achievements that make one lovable, it is one's humanity, one's weakness and need for others. Exploring one's skewed experiences and abnormalities is a prerequisite for border thinking. We can learn a lot from feminism in this work, and to me Gloria Anzaldúa is one of the most consequential and beautiful examples of such an effort. Her writings challenge us to affirm all parts of life instead of hiding behind façades—academic or otherwise.

In Sweden we have always been forced to think in another language if we want to take part in universalistic and universalizing conversations, be they in Latin, German, French, or English. As Tariq Ramadan has claimed it is "impossible to start earnest dialogue about present diversity if one persists in denying the plural reality and the diversity of one's own past, and this applies to each of the world's civilizations."[48] Precisely because we are trapped by our circumstances we need each other to understand the world, and life, better. It is because our abilities are limited that we can attach to each other and explore and see together, without having to argue that we are someone else. This is the argument made by the scientist and feminist theorist Donna Haraway in an article that has become famous for introducing the concept of "situated knowledge." Haraway's appeal for a more dialogical way of knowing has unfortunately not been given the same attention.[49]

The Moroccan philosopher Abdelkabir Khatibi talked about such a dialogical way of knowing as another thinking (*un pensée-autre*) that in his case meant thinking within both Arab and French traditions and styles without privileging any side as a starting point or merging them into a new pidgin language. Another thinking can be described as a possible result of an earnest dialogue where all participants are changed without giving up their differences.[50]

Of course it is all too easy to become rosy and naïve when talking about dialogue. Everything sounds so nice and harmonious—let's talk to each other and all will be well. Just because dialogue is theoretically possible and popular in today's multi-political environment does not mean that dialogue is always good. As Tariq Ramadan stresses: "depicting the 'dialogue of civilizations' as the positive ideology of our time to avoid discussing the strategies of political, economic, cultural, and military domination is a smokescreen and, when all is said and done, nothing but hypocrisy."

Ramadan is critical of many contemporary dialogue initiatives. The dialogues of values and ideals are a lot of empty wind, he thinks, too often offering merely symbolic recognition of other people's values that never actually touch or change the political practices that maintain injus-

---

[48] Tariq Ramadan, *Radical Reform: Islamic Ethics and Liberation*, (Oxford: Oxford University Press, 2009), 307.

[49] Donna Haraway, "Situated Knowledges: The Science Question in Feminism and the Privilege of Partial Perspective," in *Simians, Cyborgs, and Women: the Reinvention of Nature* (London: Free Association Books, 1991).

[50] Abdelkébir Khatibi, *Maghreb Pluriél*, (Paris: Denoël 1983).

tices between groups. Dialogue cannot be merely about seeing the other and letting them talk. Dialogue should instead be about coming to see our own blind spots and shortcomings, to help us understand what reforms we are in need of. Sincere dialogue must aim at self-criticism and start from a place of true respect, not from forbearing tolerance or paternalistic belief in the ability to improve other people by means of our own ideals. All too often the aim of dialogue seems to be more dialogue, rather than really addressing the issues that make dialogue necessary— that is, power, dominance and political and economic injustices. It is often said that dialogue must avoid sensitive issues. But Ramadan does not believe that such dialogues can reach to the heart of things; the risk is instead that injustices and discrimination can live on under the surface of sympathetic understanding.

I use theoretical perspectives. But I will try not to hide behind them, as theoretical reasoning should help one understand the world better and place the questions explored in a wider context. When all is said and done, the only point in understanding the world is to find my own place in it, and to try to take part in making it more inhabitable and just for all of those who are quite similar to me.

This is pretentious. Of course it is. I want to be pretentious. I also hope I can be honest and show when I am moved and affected, when I am lost and confused, without concern for what is appropriate from a scientific standpoint, or what might be seen as embarrassing.

Chapter 7

Islam in Turkey

T urkey is a special and extraordinary country. Then again, so are most countries, most probably. It is not that easy to say what has been important in shaping how Islam is lived and functions in Turkey today. I find two aspects important, though. The Turkish republic is the heir of the Ottoman Empire, whose sultan was also the caliph, who was the formal head of all of Islam. The Turkish republic is also secular, after the French model.[51] Turkish secularism is called *laiklik* in Turkish, from the French *laicite*. This version of secularism means that no religion or religious symbol whatsoever is allowed in the public sphere. For example, it was forbidden for women to wear a headscarf while attending a Turkish university until 2013. At the same time, religion is totally under the control of the secular state. The state licenses all imams and through the Directorate of Religious Affairs monitors what they preach. Such a submission of religion under the state is sometimes called Erastianism, after the Swiss 16th century theologian Erastus.

Even if religion in Turkey is controlled by the state, the role of Islam in Turkey is in some ways more like the role of Islam in the rest of Europe than it is in many other Muslim majority countries. Religion is not tied to the legitimacy of the ruling elite as is the case in many other Muslim countries.

The context of Turkish Muslims has changed dramatically in the last 80–90 years. Their state used to be the formal guardian of the Islamic

---

[51] For the main outline of Turkish history, see Erik J. Zürcher, *Turkey: A Modern History* (London: I. B. Tauris & Company, 2004).

faith, now Islam has turned into an ambivalent part of a traditionalism that the state has tried to eradicate.

Brief Turkish History

The modernization of Turkey began in the 19th century, within the Ottoman Empire. It is important to note, though, that the geographic area that was to become Turkey (mainly Anatolia) and the Turks themselves represented a minority in the Ottoman Empire. For a correct understanding of Middle Eastern history it is vital to make a distinction between the Ottoman Empire and the Republic of Turkey. Turkey did not exist until 1923, but the Turkish Republic has its prehistory in the Ottoman Empire. To refer to the Ottoman Empire as the historical Turkey leads us on the wrong track, however. The history of the Ottoman Empire is equally the history of the Balkans, of Egypt, Saudi Arabia, Libya, Lebanon, Israel and Palestine as it is the history of Turkey. From the 1840s through the 1870s, the Ottoman Empire went through the development of a constitutional rule. This development halted from 1870 until 1908. Some of the main opponents of the sultanate were a number of nationalistic movements in the outskirts of the Empire. During the latter period the sultanate reoriented its identification towards its Muslim heritage. It has been said that this was the first formation of an Ottoman nationalism, where Islam was used as a unifying symbol. The constitutional developments continued after the revolution of the Young Turks in 1908. In the beginning, it was an attempt to re-establish the Ottoman Empire, although with strong modernist influences that came mainly from France. Many Young Turks were followers of the positivist belief in science. In the newly established parliament about half of the seats were held by Turks.

The Balkan wars of 1913 were a very important course of events in the histories of both the Ottoman Empire and the Republic of Turkey. Here the Empire lost control over Macedonia, Albania and Thrace, provinces that had been part of the Empire for over 500 years—as well as being the richest provinces from where a majority of the state elite originated. It was only after these great losses that ethnic Turks for the first time in Ottoman history constituted a majority of the Empire's population.

During the First World War, when the Ottomans took part on the German side, the Empire returned to a one party rule under the Young Turks (formally known as the Committee of Union and Progress). The Committee was mainly made up of Turks from the Western parts of the Empire and was formed in Salonika, a city that is now a part of Greece under the name of Thessaloniki. Mustafa Kemal Atatürk, the father of the Turkish Republic and its symbol and guardian, came from Salonika.

After the war, large parts of the Ottoman Empire were occupied by the victorious powers. The Young Turks broke with the Sultanate and under the name of Turkish nationalism they formed a resistance movement that primarily fought the Greek occupation of Anatolia. In 1922 the Turks had gained control over most of the land that is today's Republic of Turkey.

The Anatolian Kurds and Turks of the Ottoman Empire had first of all been Muslim, contrary to Armenian Christians and Greek and Syrian Orthodox Christians. When the Armenians were expelled during the First World War, and the Greek Orthodox where moved to Greece as part of the Lausanne Treaty of 1921, the common Other was gone from the Empire. Still, it was the young republic's abolishment of the Caliphate in 1924 that lead to massive Kurdish protests as the religious symbol uniting Turks and Kurds during Ottoman times was taken away. In 1925 Kurdish revolts broke out. Some Kurds were set on creating a Kurdish nation-state, but the broader support for the revolts had religious roots.

The Republic also singled out Turkish as the only language of the state, saying that its inhabitants were Turks, and anyone who chose to speak Turkish and acknowledged the legitimacy of the state was accepted as Turkish. The nationalism of the Turkish state was not based on blood and ancestry, but on performance and identification. Most Alevites, a Shi'ite inspired Islamic tradition in Turkey that constituted and still constitutes about one fifth of the population of the new Republic, supported the secularism of the Young Turks as a way out of Sunni supremacy and oppression. The official ideology of the Republic has always been about the ideals of the state bureaucracy, and its efforts to spread these ideals in society. The position of the traditional state bureaucrats is now threatened because of the political developments during the AK Party era. This does not mean that democracy is threatened, just as it does not mean that all those opposing the old secularist elite are necessarily democratic. The outcome of the critique against AK Party that gained momentum during 2013 can most probably be interpreted as a sign for the need for a new and more inclusive deal in Turkish democracy, not as a return to a previous state.

Many still remember how Turkish militant Islamists in November 2003 bombed two synagogues, the British consulate and a British bank. Over 60 people were killed. It is said that over 450 Turkish citizens have gone through terrorist training in the al-Qaida camps in Afghanistan. There are militant Islamists also in Turkey, even if they are very marginal.

The republic of Turkey seems to be a deeply divided state. Only a couple of years ago the state security was perceived by the chief prosecutor as threatened because the wives of both the president and the prime minister wore headscarves in public. How deep is this division?

I have a Turkish friend whose name is Çağdaş. Another friend is called Muslim. Çağdaş means "modern" in Turkish. Çağdaş's parents belonged to the state bureaucracy until they retired; it was important for them to be modern and European. To show that they had left the Muslim heritage of Turkey behind them, they named their first born son "Modern." The names "Muslim" and "Modern" are a sign of the division in Turkey over the country's identity.

All throughout its 90 year history the Turkish state has identified itself as a modern European state. The official identification has been strongly secular. Many of the great reforms that president Atatürk and his parliament initiated during the 1920s were aimed at limiting Islamic presence in public spaces. The strongest reform was probably the abolishment of the Caliphate in 1924, something that can be likened to an abolishment of the Pope in Italy (even if the Caliphate's power was more symbolic than real). In 1926 the Muslim *medrese* (*madrasa*) schools were also shut down and all education was put under state control. The previous year saw the banning of male headgear such as the fez and the turban, and also the closure of socially and politically important Sufi orders. It also became forbidden to visit *türbe*s, holy men's graves.

The headscarf was not forbidden, even if some women were attacked for wearing "backward" clothing. The prohibition on the headscarf in public spaces that is still in place, even if headscarves have become informally permitted during the last years, was formulated in the constitution of the coup makers of 1980, who saw Islamists as a threat to the security they had set out to maintain. The earlier symbolic connection between nation and religion was also broken with the introduction of a Western calendar and a Latin alphabet. On the 9th of August, 1928, it was announced that a new Turkish writing system using Latin letters was to replace the Arabic and Persian letters of the Ottomans. As of the 1st of January, 1929, all official writing was to be in the new alphabet. All of this was part of a reorientation away from a symbolic fellowship with the Islamic *ummah* to an identificatory connection with European modernity.

Still, despite all the efforts to make Turkey into a modern, European state, a majority of the Turkish population has maintained its identification as Muslim and given its children names like Müslim, Ali, Fatma and Ayşe (Aisha). In this way people are born into an outlook on the identity of the country and learn to greet each other either in a Muslim manner—*selamun aleyküm*—or, if you are called Korkmaz, Çağdaş, Mebrure or Deniz, in a secular manner—*iyi günler*.

The language reforms were important parts of the modernization efforts. After a while the most purist of language ideologists came to dominate the reform works, and in the 1930s ultra-nationalistic ideas about trying to generate a totally pure Turkish language dominated. Thus "pure" Turkish alternatives to all the old religious polite courtesy phrases, to Arabic and Persian technical terminology was developed and promoted by the state elite. It isn't that easy to override people's ways of talking, though. Therefore the language used today has become an identity marker whereby the speaker shows his or her identification as Muslim or secular.

But is this really such a strong dichotomy, either—or? Can't you be a Modern European Muslim Turk?

Of course you can. A "third way" seems to be more and more navigable. The success of the ruling Justice and Development Party (Adalet ve Kalkınma Partisi, AK Party) was a telling example. The party stands on firm Muslim foundations in its work for the Turkish accession to the European Union, and for the implementation of human rights. It is hard to judge what is going on in the harsh rhetoric and power struggle Erdoğan launched in response to the Gezi protests and onwards. How deep will it affect the party and Turkish society on the whole? But I would hold that those saying "I told you so," are not entirely correct. I would argue that the democratic commitment of the AK Party was genuine, even if chairman Erdoğan slowly became more and more unwilling to challenge Turkish nationalism, and started clinging to power rather than following what he used to state as his convictions. There has also been a strand of moral conservatism with the party representatives making those that do not follow religious norms for family life and orderliness more exposed. This should not be taken as a proof for a fundamentally un-democratic tendency of the AK Party. As many Hizmet persons rightly say in response to the more authoritarian rhetoric and politics: They have changed, we have not.

The broad Nakşibendi and Nur movements are other proponents of the idea of a harmonious union of Islam and modernity. Said Nursi stated that the amalgamation of modern European science and traditional Islam would produce a new, more profound, and better civilization. Many Nur followers take their arguments from Western scientists and philosophers as well as from the Qur'an and the philosophers and theologians of Islam. To be able to live and work in a global and tolerant future where Islam and science together bring happiness, people need to be multilingual, they hold. This is one of the reasons why Gülen supporters run hundreds of schools in Turkey where English and natural sciences are on top of the priority lists. Many representatives in this movement are knowledgeable in both English and Arabic, at the same time as they are firmly rooted in their Turkish identity and their

Turkish language. Gülen has said that it is as important to study chemistry as it is to study the Qur'an.

Gülen and many other Turkish Muslims claim to uphold all the positive aspects of Europe, making the European model more durable for the future by reintroducing spirituality and the respect for God. They use a religiously colored Turkish, and many of the women wear headscarves. They have their base among the small and medium size entrepreneurs who are a driving force behind the strong economic growth of Turkey and who are coming forward as a middle class that challenges the old bureaucratic elite. Many of them are morally conservative, but at the same time more devoted to democracy than those who protect secularism with all possible means. This movement engages millions of people in Turkey. This of course means that some opportunists and people hungry for power will try to get involved.

It remains to be seen what a stronger Turkish Islamic identity will mean in the long run. I certainly think this is where the democratic process is heading, even if the representatives of the old elite together with the military have done their best to stop it. It is not democracy that they are primarily protecting; rather they uphold an idea of a modern, enlightened despot. Against this stands a partly conservative and moralistic Muslim democracy movement that has voted the AK Party to power and given them renewed confidence during the last parliamentary elections of 2011 and the regional elections in March 2014. As seen this has now developed into full scale conflict. The movement will in some ways never be the same after this, even if it survives without being prosecuted. The direct political impact of the movement proved to be very modest when only a few percent of the votes shifted from AK Party to the nationalist MHP, something that might be counted as the result of Hizmet media's argumentation. How this power struggle will turn out in the end is hard to tell, but a Muslim presence is there to stay.

During the spring of 2012 an interesting tension between AK Party and the Hizmet Movement became visible in public. The largest Turkish daily newspaper, Hizmet affiliated *Zaman*, became more openly critical of the government. Gülen and Hizmet always say they have no political aspirations. I will talk more about how this can be understood later.

Still, by its sheer size and influence the movement is drawn into politics, willingly or not. If their media is more critical of the government, what would they like to see instead? This is a valid question, and it is hard to avoid. I am sometimes troubled by how light-heartedly some Hizmet intellectuals dismiss the question of political impact with the mantra-like expression "we are not in politics." It is true that they are not tied to a certain political ideology or party. Others, like myself, have a broader definition of politics and see social movements as central in politics. Being an influential social movement means having political power, even if this is not the purpose of the movement. The new challenge for Hizmet is how to deal with those who understand that they might make political gains by attaching themselves to Hizmet. These dealings easily become political, even if people do all they can to avoid it.

The broader Islamic resurgence in Turkey that has been visible during the last 15 to 20 years does not only consist of Hizmet or *Nur*, though. There are many different shades.

The most important for many years was the National Outlook (Milli Görüş), founded and led by Necmettin Erbakan. He founded the first Islam-based party in Turkey in 1970. This party was immediately banned after the 1971 memorandum by the army. Erbakan founded a new party that was again banned by the over-throwers of 1980. During the last years of the 1970s Turkey was torn by political violence from both left and right, but not from Erbakan's party. Still, it was a meeting organized by this party that the military took as the excuse for launching its third coup on the 12th of September, 1980. Of course the party was dissolved, but Erbakan quickly came back in 1983 to form the Welfare Party (Refah Partisi) that later came to take part in the government in the mid-1990s. Erbakan was not allowed to work in peace this time either; as with all of its progenitors, the Welfare Party was charged with anti-secular activity, forced out of government and dissolved in what has come to be called the soft, or post-modern, military coup in the spring of 1997. Once again Erbakan was banned from politics. In the wake of the soft coup the Refah Party was split and the more moderate and democratic members founded the AK Party, which is in power today. In 2001

Erbakan and the Milli Görüş came back with a new party, but they only managed to win a small percent of the vote in the last few elections.

Erbakan and his supporters have been called Islamists and fundamentalists. Still, we are dealing here with a leader who for more than 40 years, through a number of different political parties, has respected the democratic order, an order that repeatedly punished him for his willingness to take part in it.

What in my eyes could be frightening with Erbakan, who died in 2011, was his tendency to think that behind every form of Western evil lay a Zionistic conspiracy trying to realize the dream of the father of the Zionist ideology—Theodor Herzl—which was to incorporate parts of Turkey in a future Great-Israel. Erbakan suspected that the European Union was part of this conspiracy. This did not prevent him from acting resolutely pragmatically and closing a military defense agreement with Israel during his term as prime minister.

The Welfare Party promised to close all city brothels and allocate separate bus lines for women, promises that were never realized. However, the banning of Erbakan and his party had nothing to do with anti-Semitism, oppression of women or economic incapability. The charge was anti-secular activity.

Today Erbakan's heritage is quite marginalized, his old party received only 1.2 percent of the vote in the elections of 2011, and his skepticism towards the European Union is not shared by his old colleagues who now run the AK Party. Through its different political phases Milli Görüş always put a lot of energy toward helping the poor and fighting corruption in the cities it governed.

Nakşibendi

In order to understand the different Islamic organizations and groups in Turkey, a historical recounting is needed. Almost all contemporary Islamic initiatives in Turkey, including Milli Görüş, spring in some way or another from the Sufi Nakşibendi tradition (Nakşibendi in Turkish and Naqshbandiyya in Arabic; the two can be used interchangeably, along with the term Naqshbandi). Also the *Nur* and the Hizmet Movements have important influences in the Nakşibendi tradition.[52]

The name comes from the 14th century sheikh Bahauddin Naqsh-band Bukhari. As can be read in his name he was active in Bukhara, in current day Uzbekistan. His order has since divided into several different branches. During the 15th and 16th centuries the Naqshbandi order developed into a worldwide organization, represented in China, India and later also in Southeast Asia, Central Asia and the Ottoman Empire. The branch that became prominent in Turkey has its roots in India, from the great Imam Rabbani Ahmad Sirhindi, who lived in Punjab around the turn of the 17th century. Imam Rabbani was called the great reviver of the second Islamic millennium (*mujaddid alf thani*) and thus the branch of Naqshbandiyya that follows him is called Mujaddidi-Naqshbandiyya.

The Turkish Nakşibendi movement is sometimes called Halidiye (Khalidiyya). It branched off from the broader Mujaddidi-Naqshbandi-yya with Sheik Khalid Baghdadi who lived in the Ottoman Empire between 1779 and 1827. Mawlana Khalid, as he is called in Turkish, was Kurdish, born near the city of Shahrazur in today's Iraq. He lived during a time when the Islamic world still had an independent educational structure. After having studied in the city of Sulaymaniyah, Mawlana Khalid continued his education by traveling to India to study under Shah Ghulam Ali in the Indian Mujaddidi-Naqshbandiyya order. On his return to Kurdistan, Mawlana Khalid was named representative (*khalifa*) for the Mujaddidi order. He met resistance from the other established Sufi orders in the region and therefore first moved to Baghdad, then to Damascus, cities that both were within the Ottoman Empire. Mawlana Khalid won many followers and today all Nakşibendi groups in Turkey count him as part of their lineage (*silsila*).

The Nakşibendi teaching has always promoted social engagement, and one of its main principles is solitude within society, that one is with God even among people (*khalwat dar anjuman*). The peace one seeks

---

[52] On Nakşibendi: Emin Yaşar Demirci, *Modernisation, Religion and Politics in Turkey: The Case of the Iskenderpasa Community* (İstanbul: İnsan Publications, 2008), and Elisabeth Özdalga (ed.), *Naqshbandis in Western and Central Asia* (İstanbul: Swedish Research Institute, 1999).

in the nearness of God must not be at the expense of the responsibility to take part in society, to be political. Many of the most important representatives, not the least Imam Rabbani, have stressed and observed this double responsibility and been active in society. Mawlana Khalid even urged his followers to pray for the Ottoman state that was pressured by several nationalistic insurgencies around the empire, by Christian missionaries and by Wahhabi criticism.

Several different factors in the Nakşibendi practice made its members well adapted to the modern social environment. Their Sufi service (*dhikr*—recitation of one or some of God's Names) did not require them to gather in seclusion, and it did not contain any spectacular parts. Nakşibendi ritual, *dhikr* (*zikir* in Turkish), is most often quiet and individual. Even though Nakşibendi adherents were not dependent on meeting halls for their spiritual practice, there were more Nakşibendi lodges (*tekke*) than there were for any other order when the modern Turkish state banned Sufi orders in 1925. Nakşibendi adapted much more easily to a life in seclusion than other orders. Even if they were limited in their movements by the ban, they continued to have great influence. From 1980 onwards a number of media outlets were established, and some Nakşibendi members came to seek employment in the Presidency of Religious Affairs (*Diyanet*) that controls Islam in Turkey, a kind of underground internal colonization. The most important Nakşibendi leader (*shaikh*) who influenced most of the first generation of Islamic politicians in the modern Republic was the imam in the İskenderpaşa mosque, Mehmet Zaid Kotku (1897–1980). In the İskenderpaşa mosque he came to influence not only Necmettin Erbakan, but also future prime minister and president Turgut Özal, prime minister Recep Tayyip Erdoğan, and ministers Lütfü Doğan, Fehim Adak and Korkut Özal. İskenderpaşa is still one of the dominating Nakşibendi groups in Turkey, with strong financial resources that fund several media companies, among other things. Radio broadcasts have been an important way for the Nakşibendi representatives to reach their followers. The İskenderpaşa representatives encourage their sympathizers to learn foreign languages, to use technology and to travel abroad to educate themselves. They are very positive towards commerce as a means to generate community and peace, and encourage their followers to open schools, hospitals, TV stations and other businesses that can improve society.

It was no coincidence that the first openly religious prime minister and president of the republic of Turkey, Turgut Özal, was a Nakşıbendi.

Another important group in Muslim Turkey is the Süleymancı movement, founded by Süleyman Hilmi Tunahan (1888–1959). It is one of the oldest religious groups in Turkey, and Tunahan also came out of the Nakşibendi tradition. Like other groups, the Süleymancı focuses on individual spirituality and supports student dormitories and boarding schools. It has also directed a large part of its activism towards financing mosques and Qur'an courses. Among Turks in the European diaspora this group has had quite a large influence. According to some, it has played a political role by counterbalancing communist influence, and as such has been used by the ruling parties. But it has never been engaged in direct political actions.

Other important Nakşıbendi groups are the Erenköy and the Işık orders. Erenköy are by some commentators counted as the strongest group today, in large part thanks to the influential leader Mahmut Sami Ramazanoğlu who until his death in 1984 influenced a number of intellectuals and businessmen. During the 1990s, Erenköy put aside more openly political interests and directed its activities to the broader civil society, where it supported charity foundations, schools, and media outlets.

The Işık Movement is an interesting example of the independent educational traditions found in the Islamic world. Işık stems from the old Nakşıbendi Kashgari logde, founded in İstanbul in the middle of the 18th century by Sheik Nidai from Kashgar in East Turkestan, modern day Xingjiang, China. Via travels to Samarkand, Aleppo, Jerusalem, Mecca, and Medina, Nidai arrived in the Ottoman capital and settled there. His example shows how the Nakşıbendi order was a contact zone for Muslims from China, Central Asia, India and the Ottoman Empire. Another tekke founder in İstanbul was Shah Khaydar of Tashkent from Uzbekistan who, after extensive travels throughout Europe, Ethiopia, and Arabia, settled in Üsküdar on the Asian shore of İstanbul. The notion of a stalled and sleeping Islamic tradition after the medieval Golden period finds little support in actual history. All the different educational routes that for centuries led to Ottoman İstanbul are vital for a sound understanding of today's modern Turkey.

A much smaller movement, but one that is much talked about, especially in Germany, is the Kaplancılar. Their leader Cemalettin Kaplan is
now imprisoned in Turkey for anti-secular activities. The Kaplan Movement has strived to make Islam and *sharia* law the basis for society. During a short period it was said to have influence over some 50 mosques
in Germany, and was banned by the German authorities in 2001. Today
the Kaplancılar are a marginal and militant group which believes that
violence is a means for creating an Islamic state in Turkey.

Yet another small group is the Haydar Baş, who goes under the name
of their founder. This movement springs from the Sufi Qadiriyya order.
They hold that dialogue with Christians and Jews is a threat to an Islamic identity, at the same time as they have a strongly nationalistic message
that they have tried to implement via their marginal political party
Bağımsız Türkiye (Independent Turkey), which got around half a percent of the vote in the 2007 elections, and even less in 2011. Despite
an almost indistinguishable political impact this movement also stands
behind a number of business investments and has also founded a few
schools.

In addition to all these groups there are others who use Islamic
symbolism and rhetoric to secure a place in the public sphere and in politics. The changes that can be seen in the Turkish public sphere thus have
deep roots in an Islamic civil society that traditionally has been formed
largely by the Sufi orders. It also has strong ties to European Muslims
in many countries. Milli Görüş, Süleymancı, Nur and Hizmet are strong
in many Turkish diaspora groups. It seems that the Hizmet Movement
with its local initiatives for dialogue and tolerance is becoming more
and more dominant.

We should not be led to believe that major antagonism in European societies lies between Muslims and modern democrats, whether in
Turkey, Holland, Denmark or Sweden. The world view spread by populist parties like the British National Party, Dutch Freedom Party, the
Danish People's Party or the Swedish Democrats is a malicious fantasy
where Muslims are reduced from living individuals into symbols for
everything these parties see as not fitting into their own nations—a Muslim, for them, is per definition someone who has no place in a European nation. I do not agree.

Chapter 8

A Meeting in İstanbul,
a Rainy Day in March

When I realized that it was time for me to get a better understanding of the Nur tradition, I went to İstanbul to get a hold of some material. I had come to understand that it all started with the Kurdish imam Bediüzzaman Said Nursi, and that Gülen was the one most writers saw as the main carrier of his ideas today. Maybe because I was trained as a historian of ideas, I thought it was best to start at the source. On the net I had found quite a few texts by both Said Nursi and Gülen. In order to get closer to them I wanted to have them as books, to be able to take notes, underline—work with the texts.

I e-mailed people at a few of the addresses I had found on various home pages of publishers and organizations based in İstanbul, and asked if I could come to visit them to learn more about Said Nursi and Gülen. As is often the case with addresses found on Turkish webpages, I did not get any replies. Eventually, a man called Ferhat answered and welcomed me to have lunch at the Journalists and Writers Foundation (JWF) together with the Vice President Cemal Uşşak.

When it came to Said Nursi, I had to make do with an address to the publishing house that published the English translations made by Şükran Vahide, who used to be called Mary Weld and lives in England.

The main purpose of my visit to Turkey this time was to meet representatives of the Turkish branch of Amnesty International, and together with them and friends from Amnesty Sweden, plan a mutual project funded by the Swedish Olof Palme Center. We were also to take part in a program on women's rights on International Women's day, the 8th of March.

I came down to İstanbul a few days before to have time to look for Said Nursi and Gülen material. As always, my double errands took me to very different areas of İstanbul life. The human rights activists I met were not religious, and the opposite sides of Turkish society became visible, even if the offices of the Journalists and Writers Foundation and Amnesty were only ten-minute walk from each other. Spring was in the air in the afternoon I landed. I could already take my winter jacket off at the airport. As is often the case when I travel to Turkey, my bag was light; I hoped to fill my weight quota with books on the return flight. I arrived in the city center in the late afternoon. I jumped off the tram at Eminönü and walked out on the Galata Bridge, thinking about walking all the way up to Arya Hotel, which is located in a small alleyway at the lower end of İstiklal Street. I found it too hot, though, and decided to take the old 19th century underground up the hill.

The following morning it was colder, and it rained. As happens when it rains in central İstanbul I didn't have to walk more than a block before I found an umbrella seller. I bought a model in green see-through plastic for five liras. The color suited the Islamic program of my day, I thought.

The publisher's address was Sorkun Han, a commercial building. These commercial buildings are often made up of a central courtyard with several stories in the surrounding houses. I hadn't been able to find the exact address on my maps (and I was not yet familiar with Google maps), but the Cağaloğlu district where it was located is relatively small and I felt I knew it reasonably well, as it sits between the historical tourism magnets and the covered bazaars. I hoped to easily ask my way there once I was in the area. As I hadn't had any response to my emails, I was uncertain what I would find. I walked up the hill on Ankara Street from the European train station and started by checking the books at the many small publishers and book shops there. As I came to the corner where Ankara Street meets Nuruosmaniye Street, I stopped to think, and decided to turn right towards the bazaars and try to ask my way on from there. After almost half an hour of squelching along the wet pavement, I was back on the corner where I started. No one had known where

Sorkun Han was. I decided to check out what they had in stock in Diyanet's religious book shop, which lies on that corner. I found a few English titles by a professor named Nureddin Uzunoğlu, among others a translation of the Qur'an.

This dedicated writer and missionary is unfortunately rather mediocre in English and his text was often difficult to follow. He lives in the USA. I am puzzled that he and his publishers think that the cause of Islam is furthered by these almost unreadable books. Who has decided to publish them? Maybe he finances them himself? Anyway, I bought a history of the Prophets mentioned in the Qur'an and a book about the meaning of God's 99 Names.

When I came out on the stairs and stopped to wonder where I should turn next, I saw the logo of the publisher I was looking for on a sign just across the junction, on a balcony on the second floor.

The stairwell was very modest and insignificant, piled up with cardboard boxes, and no signs telling who lived or worked in the building. I went up to the second floor and knocked on a door I presumed lead to the balcony I had spotted. A man opened, and I asked if this happened to be the publisher I was looking for, and if he possibly spoke English. Yes, it was the publisher, but he did not speak English. I had to carry on with my somewhat flatfooted Turkish.

The man invited me inside, where the floors were covered with wall-to-wall carpets. I took of my wet shoes and went in. One room had two desks with telephones; the other was traditionally furnished only along the walls. Divans were placed under the windows, and the other walls were covered with shelves where all of Said Nursi's books stood with the covers facing outwards—in Turkish, Arabic, English, German and a dozen other languages.

Naturally I was offered tea and my host was very happy and interested in me coming from Sweden. How had I found my way here? How did I know Said Nursi? What languages could I read? And a couple of other questions I could not fully understand.

Had I known then that I was going to write this book, in this way, I would have made sure to remember his name. Now I can only think that I remember that he was called İbrahim. This is the way it is, in any research process—and in life—no matter how thorough and well planned you are, you will eventually always shift your focus and realize you haven't done all that you should have. When İbrahim and I had calmly drunken our tea, talked about the weather and praised the fact that I had found them at last, I went over to the book shelves and started botanizing.

From much I could recognize from the internet, Said Nursi's *oeuvre* is not easily overviewed. Almost everything he wrote is collected in the *Risale-i Nur*—around 6,000 pages of letters, Qur'anic exegeses, meditations, stories, sermons, and other thematic writings. Much of what he wrote is also published in other contexts, as leaflets directed towards different occasions and readers. The separate text, *A Guide to the Youth*, is also a part of the larger collection *The Words*, and so on.

I took the four central volumes of the *Risale-i Nur* and a couple of what I saw as the most important smaller publications, all in English. The original Turkish written by Said Nursi is complicated even for many native Turkish readers. His mother tongue was Kurdish; his first language of writing was Arabic, followed by Persian. It was only in his 20's that he learned Turkish, and only a few years after this he started writing in Turkish. He never accepted writing Turkish with the new Latin alphabet until in 1956, though. He claimed that this would distance the language from its place in the Muslim community, which was part of the purpose of the reformists. Said Nursi's Turkish remained filled with words and expressions of Arabic and Persian origin.

When İbrahim realized I was a researcher, he insisted that I must speak with persons who could help me along the way in my studies, and who could answer my questions accurately. First he rang Şükran Vahide, whose biography of Said Nursi I had read, and whom I knew to be the main English translator of the *Risale-i Nur*. The contact was a bit abrupt, for both me and Mrs. Vahide, and I did not manage to come up with any clever questions. As this conversation quickly came to an end, we both felt somewhat awkward, and thought I should talk to someone more. Now I rang Faris Kaya, director at İstanbul Foundation for Science and Culture. Kaya was enthusiastic about my interest. He thought we should meet before I started truly digging into the reading. When we realized we could not find any time for a meeting this time he invited me to a workshop the coming autumn and said, with strong emphasis, that if I wondered about anything whatsoever as I read Said Nursi I should promise to call him directly, no matter what the time. I got his work number, home number and e-mail address.

Whenever I have emailed him, he has always answered promptly, in detail and with friendly follow-up questions. When I have attended conferences and workshops, he is the main player, always finding time to pat everyone on the back and arrange a meeting, if only for half a minute. He is large, loud, with the neck of a bull and a grey mustache. He is of the constitution that is not made to wear a suit, but does it anyway. He reminds me of a picture of the romantic philosopher Fichte in one of my philosophy textbooks at university. Faris is physical in his contact with people; he often high fives with women in order not to be too intimate.

He is an overwhelming person, a doer. I cannot understand how he finds the peace and time to read, but somehow he has managed to indulge in most of what is worth knowing about Said Nursi. While I am still thinking about my view on a particular question raised, Faris has had time to move on and meet eleven other of his friends.

Anyway, I got my books neatly wrapped in a package, thanked İbrahim for the tea and commitment, and went back out in the rain.

Chapter 9

Said Nursi, Jaques Derrida and the Limits of Justice

As has been said, there are some affinities between the post-modern critiques of positivist modernity that have formed the research contexts I have worked in, and the critiques of the same modernity within Islam, by Nur thinkers and others.

From my perspective the French-Algerian philosopher Jacques Derrida is the most important representative of postmodern philosophy; he might even be the most important thinker of the late 20th century.

My first contribution on Said Nursi was to compare the views on worldly justice in Derrida and Said Nursi. I wrote an article for the International Symposium for Said Nursi Studies that is held every third year by the İstanbul Foundation for Science and Culture. The symposium, which brought together over one hundred researchers, was held in October 2007 in Kumburgaz, an empty seaside resort at the Marmara sea closed down during the winter, only an hour to the west of İstanbul. The participants came from Turkey, Great Britain, USA, Canada, Malaysia, Indonesia, the Philippines, Russia, Bosnia, Jordan, Morocco, Nigeria, Saudi Arabia, Germany, Italy, Egypt, Turkmenistan, and a number of other countries. "True Justice is Beyond the Reach of Modernistic Reason" was the title of my presentation. "Man, whose life is so brief, cannot experience the true essence of justice in this transient world; [...] this passing and transient world is far from manifesting such wisdom and justice for man."[53]

---

[53] Bediüzzaman Said Nursi, *The Words: On the Nature and Purposes of Man, Life and All Things, From the Risale-i Nur Collection 1*, (İstanbul: Sözler Publications, 2004) 78.

Thus said the Kurdish Islamic thinker Bediüzzaman Said Nursi in the little Turkish village of Barla in 1925. At the Cardozo Law School in metropolitan New York in the autumn of 1989 the French postmodern philosopher Jacques Derrida said:

> Justice is incalculable, it requires us to calculate with the incalcula-ble; and aporetic experiences are the experiences, as improbable as they are necessary, of justice, that is to say of moments in which the decision between just and unjust is never insured by a rule.[54]

Their remarks are in some senses compatible, in content if not in their style of expression. Derrida's argument is as always wrapped in a careful, if not always direct, style. Said Nursi is a preacher that likes to talk with big words and wide gestures. The claim for similarity might therefore be surprising, given that these quotes come from two men of very different surroundings and circumstances. If we see beyond the apparent differences, both men talk about a world where we will never meet true justice, a volatile world that is opaque in front of reason. We can never know what is truly just, we can only hope. There is no way to decide if the law is just.

Said Nursi is often described as critical of philosophy. In many of his writings he says that conflict stands between religion and philoso-phy. It is very important to read these remarks in the context of the time in which they were formulated. Those who talked about their view of society as philosophical in the social circles Said Nursi frequented were mostly the Young Turk nationalists, deeply influenced by French posi-tivism and set on replacing the religious society with a scientific one. Another front stood against the highly rationalistic Aristotelian phil-osophical tradition within Islam, which Said Nursi had studied but found too much driven by the mind, at the price of the heart and senses. In a late text, like *The Staff of Moses,* Said Nursi himself stresses that it is not philosophy as such that he challenges, but the philosophy that thinks

---

[54] Jacques Derrida, "Force of Law: The "Mystical Foundation of Authority,'" in *Deconstruction and the Possibility of Justice*, Drucilla Cornell, Michel Rosenfeld and David Gray Carlson (ed.), (New York: Routledge, 1992) 16.

itself self-sufficient and that comes to materialistic conclusions—and thus denies God.

One of the things I wanted to get through to the Said Nursi researchers and readers was that contemporary continental philosophy is something rather different from the philosophy under critique in the *Risale-i Nur*. In my reading they both criticize the same over-confident belief in the reach of reason, but from different angles. It could be called before and after, or from the outside and the inside. Said Nursi's arguments come from sources unknown to the positivists. Derrida dedicated his philosophical life to the opening of holes in the core of Western tradition to show how the texts that have been used to legitimize strong rationalism have blind spots and have overlooked assumptions that undermine positivist positions.

As said, Said Nursi's discussions on Islam and Western philosophy are closely tied to the specific circumstances of the late Ottoman Empire and early republican Turkey. Within the field of Western philosophy there are many new traditions and styles born after Said Nursi's time that share in the critique of positivistic philosophy and modernist Western civilization that Said Nursi formulated. This means that there is room for dialogue and some recognition of the other's related work from these two sides. This is of course also an argument meant to challenge all those who claim that East is East and West is West, and that there exists a fundamental, inalienable difference between the Western and the Islamic civilizations.

My point was—and is—that the dividing line is not between the East and the West; there are many possibilities for working together and finding support for the development of a more humble relation to nature and our fellow men, what some call Creation.

My choice of Derrida as a point of comparison was not only because he had formulated some of the cornerstones of my own world view. "Derrida's name has probably been mentioned more frequently in books, journals, lectures, and common-room conversations during the last 30 years than that of any other living thinker," wrote *The Guardian* in his obituary.

For me it was also an opportunity to argue for the importance of personal experience in the formation of any person's thinking. Derrida's critique of Western modernity was not only intellectual or philosophical, it also stemmed from a sense of exclusion that made him more acutely aware of the discrepancies between modernist rhetoric and action.

Derrida as an Algerian Jew

Derrida, who died in 2004 at the age of 74, was of Algerian Jewish decent. Robert Young has argued that rather than some philosophical vogue in Paris, it was the French atrocities in Algeria that gave birth to postmodernism. Derrida was educated in French culture at the same time as the French colonial rule in Algeria turned into war, a war eventually won by the Algerians. The rift between rhetoric and action was deep and acute. But I think Derrida's earlier confrontation with a harsh and widespread anti-Semitism in French Algeria during the Second World War was even more formative and important in regard to his views on Western civilization. He had suffered beatings in the streets, insults for being a "dirty Jew," and in 1942 he was barred from school for almost a year solely because of his alleged Jewishness. A Jewish identification was forced upon him by the Vichy regime, even though he came from a family that self-identified as French. Had he lived his youth in a different setting, Jewishness might never have become an issue for him.[55]

In Algeria, as in all colonial places, it became violently clear that Western modernity did not only mean the declaration of human rights and a belief in democracy; it was also a deadly idea used to restrict those rights to Westerners only. In the words of Anne McClintock:

> Imperialism is not something that happened elsewhere—a disagreeable fact of history external to Western identity. Rather, imperialism and the invention of race were fundamental aspects of Western, industrial modernity.[56]

---

[55]   Jason Powell, *Jacques Derrida: a Biography* (New York: Continuum, 2006).
[56]   McClintock, Anne, *Imperial Leather: Race, Gender and Sexuality in the Colonial Contest*, (New York: Routledge, 1995) 5.

Post-colonial Studies: A Derridian Offspring

McClintock can be called a postmodern, postcolonial thinker. A common ground for postcolonial studies, very much inspired by Derrida, is a critique of the scientific belief in the possibility of a full and objective knowledge of man. The established scientific knowledge of man and his role in the world has been formulated in the West; this knowledge has often been used to justify geopolitical injustices. A clear formulation of this view can be found in Edward Said's important book *Culture and Imperialism*. In that book Said says that even the high culture of Western modernity, such as the novels of Jane Austen or the operas of Verdi, is closely linked and dependent on colonial imperialism. The "Progress" and "Development" of the West can never be fully understood without a simultaneous consideration of the oppression of the rest of the world that took place at the same time and according to the same foundational ideas. The non-Western world has had to play the role of total opposite and Other to the West. That means that what in positivistic modernity has been viewed as objective scientific knowledge of the inhabitants of other parts of the world is tainted by colonial power.

Modern empiricism said that if people turned out to be different and thus "inferior," that had to be accepted. And since empirical observations very often took the white middle aged male as a norm, non-Westerners and women appeared to be different and therefore inferior.

Said Nursi as an Ottoman Kurd

Said Nursi was born in 1877 in Bitlis province, in a rather ordinary family that in Şükran Vahide's words "were among the settled Kurdish population of the geographical region the

Ottomans called Kurdistan."[57] For the same purpose that I stressed the Jewishness of Derrida, I want to lay weight on the Kurdishness of Said Nursi.

During the reign of the Young Turks Committee of Union and Progress, Said Nursi, also known as Said Kurdi, lobbied for the educational

---

[57] Şükran Vahide, *Islam in Modern Turkey: An Intellectual Biography of Bediüzzaman Said Nursi*, (Albany: SUNY Press, 2005) 3.

rights of Kurdish children in the East, who dressed in traditional Kurdish garb. His straightforward and uncourtly manners got him arrested and sent to a mental asylum. At one instance (in "The Fourteenth Ray"[58]) he quotes a former governor who tried to scare away his friends by picking on the fact that he was a Kurd and a follower of the Shafi legal school, different from the Hanafi Turks. To reach out in İstanbul he had started communicating in Ottoman Turkish, his fourth language after Kurdish, Arabic and Persian, which he from then on used as the vehicle for his teachings. Still, he faced suspicion because of his Kurdish origins. A full association with a Western reformist identity was never possible for him, and when the Republic opted for Turkish modernization in opposition to Islam he was sent into "compulsory residence" in various locations decided by the Republican regime until the coming to power of Adnan Menderes and the Democratic Party in the 1950s. Said Nursi died in 1960.

Said Nursi's critique of the Ottoman modernization program Tanzimat and the Young Turks' Turkism, and his own views on progressive reforms as de-Islamification, have at least one foot in Kurdistan, always viewed as backward. One can find different layers of experiences of coloniality in Said Nursi's biography.

Said Nursi and the Critique of Modernity and Colonialism

Colonialism is fundamental to modernity and therefore it affects not only former colonizers or colonized peoples, but also has deep effects on all countries, not the least those, such as my own home country Sweden or Said Nursi's Turkey, which have enrolled in modernity. This vaguer but broader effect of colonialism is covered by the concept coloniality, coined as an equivalent of modernity, to stress that the effects of colonialism is much wider than its effects in actual colonies. Mücahit Bilici has described "Kemalist modernization in Turkey by the state [...] as cultural self-colonization."[59] Said Nursi called its supporters "pseudo-patriotic

---

[58] Said Nursi, *The Rays*, (İstanbul: Sözler Neşriyat, 2002), pp. 327–348.

[59] Mücahit Bilici, "Forgetting Gramsci and Remembering Nursi: Parallel Theories of Gramsci and Said Nursi in the Space of Eurocentrism" in Ibahim Abu-Rabi (red.),

irreligious deviants who hid under the veil of Turkism and in reality are the enemies of the Turks."[60] He made a distinction between Turkish nationalism, which could include him as a Kurd united by religion with true Turks, and the Turkism upheld by the imitators of Europe.

The history of the West in the West has for too long been written only from an inside perspective. It is our revered ideas, the basis of our identity and our history that all too often have been glorified. As long as only those who benefited from the spread of modernity were invited to write its history, the idea of what modernity meant was very much blind to all its dark sides.

In time, less colonized people from the peripheries of modernity made their way into the metropolitan centers and their experiences resulted in very different stories being told.

This happened on a broader scale in the 1960s. That was also the time when the environmental downsides of modernity's techno-scientific spread started to show. Pesticides and the exploitation of natural resources had catastrophical effects on nature. To more and more people of the West, it became obvious that the confident trust in Western man's abilities to rationally control the world was somewhat arrogant, and that modernization could be dangerous and even lethal in the longer run.

These critiques struck at the very heart of positivistic modernity. The critique could no longer be said to be just religious irrationalism or reactionary opposition to Development. But still, most Western academics would only listen to voices trained in their own tongue. In the last few decades, more and more people are starting to realize that a similar critique has been present all along in the parts of the world that suffered from the colonial spread of modernity.

Said Nursi is one of those earlier critics from the borderlands of modernity.

Islam at the Crossroads: On the Life and Thought of Bediuzzaman Said Nursi (Albany: SUNY Press, 2003).

[60] Bediüzzaman Said Nursi, *Letters: 1928–1932, From the Risale-i Nur Collection 2*, (İstanbul: Sözler Publications, 2001) 492.

The global spread of industrialism and modernity took place at the same time as the colonial imperialism that Eric Hobsbawm, in his influential *The Age of Empire,* dates to the period between 1875 and 1914. The link between colonialism and modernity is no mere coincidence. The modern capitalistic world system, built with resources from the exploitations made by European colonial imperialism, is a foundational part of modernity. Persons like Said Nursi, growing up in an unprivileged part of an Empire under constant defeat from European powers, were more likely to meet the colonial practices of the West than most Western historians and philosophers who tasted only its sweet fruits.

I think there is something to what Mücahit Bilici has argued about the similarities between Said Nursi and Italian Marxist Antonio Gramsci. But I would also like to stress differences related to Said Nursi's belonging to a strong alternative to Modernistic Europe; even if he came from a Kurdish marginality, he was an Ottoman imperial official and military volunteer as well as an Islamic scholar. He could have opted for a blank rejection of European modernity—a possibility not open to someone like Gramsci.

There is a long tradition of critique from within the margins of modernity. Gramsci brings a political one from the imperial heydays; Derrida, a philosophical one from the postcolonial era. Bilici argues that we who come from within those margins of modernity must acknowledge and highlight those outside critiques, like Said Nursi's, that carry similar messages. But we must not subsume those outside voices into simply a different shade of our own color. If we draw too hard on the similarities, the non-Western thinkers will come forward as mere imitators, or not fully developed versions of Western postmodern critique.

There are affinities in the different strands of critique against modernity that exists, and have existed, around the world. There are also certain elements that seem to be present almost everywhere. One is the critique of the one-dimensional understanding of man and nature in positivistic modernity. This would imply that there is something of importance in the argument that a positivistic and self-assured modernism lacks respect for the limitations of its beloved reason.

The world is far more complex and sensitive than techno-scientific progressivists have been able to see. The self-assured trust in modernization has led to very serious conditions on our earth. Techno-science must be held in check by something. That is a conclusion that many different people have drawn from looking back at the 20th century. What this something ought to be seems to be much more difficult to reach agreement on. When it comes to the formulation of alternatives, Said Nursi and Derrida aren't very close. And it is difficult to see that Derrida has any clear positive alternative.

There are similarities in the different critiques of positivistic, modernistic belief in a just social order based on scientific methods. These different traditions and fields might also find inspiration and support from the other critiques that approach the problem from different angles. This fact must not lead to the assumption that the different critics all strive for the same goals.

From an Islamic perspective one can distinguish between three types of reason—human, Prophetic and Divine. Complete Justice is possible only for God and the Prophets. There is a range of positions on how to view the possibilities to apply true divine justice in this world. In the settlements after the battle of Siffin in 657, the Kharijites criticized Caliph Ali for his decision to let his dispute with his opponent Muawiya be settled by arbitrators. They argued that a judgment was for God alone, and that men should not try to settle what only God could judge. Said Nursi is of course no Kharijite, but in a discussion of the wars in Ali's times in "The Fifteenth Letter," Said Nursi seems to come to the conclusion that both Muawiya and Ali could only strive for relative justice. In the political realities of this world no one can apply pure justice; the decisions will always be tainted by politics and turned into a choice of the lesser evil. Spiritual and worldly rule cannot be combined. But this fact must not lead to extremist stances like the Kharijites', Nursi stressed.[61]

On the topics of Prophetic and divine justice Derrida has nothing whatsoever to say. His hope for a better future is a more Jewish one,

---

[61]   Said Nursi, *Letters*, 74, and *The Flashes Collection, From the Risale-i Nur Collection 3*, (İstanbul: Sözler Publications, 2004) 131.

and much more agnostic—we can only keep the possibility open and wait and see. One day we will know. The exploration of similarities between Said Nursi and Derrida concerns only the human level.

The Metaphysics of Presence

One of the starting points in Derrida's extensive writings is the critique of what he calls the metaphysics of presence. Scientific objectivity rests on an assumption that it is possible to get an objective view of reality. But from where does the scientific witness observe reality? Can man really be present in an observable reality? The scientific trust in the observability of the world is metaphysical, Derrida claims.

There is no privileged or obvious presence in time or space from where man and his reason can see, understand and explain the world. Derrida argues that reality is always in motion, and that time therefore always is out of joint. It is impossible to find any place, any restricted present, where the observer can come to rest and from where he could see and understand the world. As soon as one tries to rest in a present *now*, a displacement takes place, time runs away from the observer and a difference between a time just past and the present arises. This means that it is impossible to make a difference between a real presence in a present and a representation of a present that has just passed.[62]

We can therefore never understand what reality is or who we are; at best, we might see what was, and who we were, a moment ago. Understanding always lags behind, since the circumstances we try to understand have always already changed. That means that objective observation and positivistic understanding are ultimately impossible. Reason is always belated and the world is too rich and complex to be fully observed or understood by reason. This also means that any decision will always rest on a limited analysis of a situation that is no longer present.

This argument on human reason could be seen as compatible with the view held by Said Nursi, and religious critics of philosophy in gen-

---

[62] Jacques Derrida, *La Voix et le phénomène: Introduction au problème du signe dans la phénoménologie de Husserl* (Paris: Presses Universitaires de France, 1967) chapter 4–5.

eral; man is not a self-sufficient animal but a creature that on its own is impotent, weak, poor, and in need. For Nursi and other religious thinkers this shows our deep need for humility and religious guidance. And as Said Nursi argues, for example in "The Tenth Word," there is lots of proof for the believer that there is divine justice in the Hereafter. "Since man is not called to account and judged in fitting fashion while in this world, it follows that he must proceed to a Supreme Tribunal and a final felicity."

Justice according to Derrida

For Derrida, a certain humbleness is crucial. We must realize that philosophy or science can never decide what is just. But according to Derrida the inescapable disjointedness of time makes justice a *possible* ideal and a *possible* way of behaving towards others. Every moment is in a fundamental way always open, and any experience can never be more certain than a maybe. This means that we always have a choice, and therefore we are always responsible for that choice. We cannot say that it was the only reasonable way to act. Reason isn't conclusive. Since it is impossible to know for sure, laws can never be complete or decided to be just. Derrida speaks of justice as "a messianic hope" that is always unfulfilled in this world. True justice is a problem beyond the reach of philosophy and jurisprudence. That means that the laws governing a state can never be proven to be just, they can only be legitimate or not. Justice in this world can never be more than a promise and a hope.

Derrida's argument for the incompleteness of worldly justice is compatible with Nursi's view.

But Derrida is agnostic about the possibility of the divine justice that lies at the heart of Nursi's argument.

Said Nursi meant that modern civilization was built on force, egoism, conflict, racialism and hedonism. We have already seen that postcolonial critiques hold similar views. But one thing can be elaborated on further, since it is a prominent feature in both Derrida's and Said Nursi's theories of justice—namely *force*.

Force and Legitimacy: Derrida and Nursi

A law of course needs to be enforced to have any relevance. To discuss this aspect of justice,

Derrida elaborates on the German philosophers Immanuel Kant and Walter Benjamin, who both expressed the view that there can be no worldly justice without force. But where is the line between this unavoidable use of force to uphold the law and unjust violence? That is one of the major questions in Derrida's text. Is there a non-violent force?

To say "I am just!" or "This is just" is to betray justice, Derrida says. We cannot know what is just, and to enforce what is not just is an act of violence. As long as modern civilization rests on a firm belief in the conclusiveness of reason, it will rest on a violent force. "Modern civilization's [...] point of support is force," says Said Nursi. Derrida and Said Nursi can be read as supporting each other on that point. But Derrida goes on to say that justice without force is not possible either. Justice that has no power to be enforced is no justice. Nursi would probably argue that God is the All-Powerful and All-Just, and that it is only at the level of divine justice that the problem can be solved. But when he stood in the courts of the Turkish

Republic defending the *Risale-i Nur*, his friends and himself, he was facing this very problem and addressed it. In the Afyon court he defended himself and at one point said in response to all the harassments he had had to suffer: "Is it not unprecedented tyranny in the name of justice? Is it not an unprecedented miscarriage of justice on account of the law?"[63]

Derrida would say that the law can never be just, or at least we can never decide if it is in accord with justice. In a context where divine revelation is not a valid argument, we have no way to decide, so we can't expect or demand that the law shall be just. We can only demand that it should be legitimate. And that is precisely the argument followed by Nursi when he was persecuted, probably because he understood that an argument from revelation or the Qur'an would not be

---

[63] Said Nursi, *The Rays*, (İstanbul: Sözler Neşriyat, 2002), 455.

considered valid; it would rather have been seen as a proof of his guilt. In addressing the Afyon court he reviewed his case from the principles of the Republic. The

Republic embraces a principle of freedom of conscience that must be applied also to the students of the *Risale-i Nur*, he argues. A conviction in the case could not be legitimate, as it would show that the court rulings of the Republic are not in accordance with the principles it itself says it embraces. Whether those principles are just or not might be another question.

Even one who finds them not to be just can demand that the laws shall be legitimate and upheld. "I want my rights within the bounds of the law. I accuse of being criminals those who act against the law in the name of the law. The laws of the Government of the Republic certainly reject the arbitrary acts of such criminals. I am hopeful that my rights will be restored to me."[64]

Against Positivism, in Different Ways

Mücahit Bilici demands the recognition of Said Nursi's, and other non-Western intellectuals', contribution to the critique of modernity. I would agree that reading Said Nursi gives a fuller and more elaborated understanding of Western modernity. I would also argue that a reader of Said Nursi can get a fuller and more elaborated understanding of modernity and worldly justice by reading Jacques Derrida.

There are interesting similarities in the critique of positivistic philosophy in these two writers.

Both are anti-dualistic and deeply suspicious of the dichotomy of tradition versus modernity.

Derrida will often try to show that the shady place in between the clear sides of a dichotomy cannot and should not be eliminated by definitions or rational precision. The world is more grayish than it is black and white. Most often there is good and bad in every option. Nursi does not, as is all too common, set up a choice between Islam and moderni-

---

[64]   Ibid.

ty. His way ahead is in a blend of the two sides that is truer and more original, more Islamic. Said Nursi's differentiation between two different views of Europe is a well-known example. He is no rough critic of Europe who says everything European is sinful or bad. Rather he sees a true civilization in Europe that needs to be recovered in the name of justice and right. In a similar way, Derrida is searching for a truer use of the European philosophical legacy. Derrida's translator and post-colonial critic Gayatri Chakravorty Spivak has said that Derrida's method of deconstruction is a persistent critique of what one cannot not want. I think the phrase is suitable also for Said Nursi's relation to modern scientific enterprises.

Said Nursi and Derrida are not new age mystics who feel contempt for reason or science. They are criticizing those who use reason as an argument for oppression, and they both do it in the name of a higher reasonability. But at that point it also becomes clear how big the differences are between one who has only a vague messianic hope that such a pure reason does exist, and one who stands firm in the belief in revelation and a supreme tribunal.

Derrida's religion is a very opaque monotheism bereft of any revelation. There is nothing higher than reason, but there are all too many who think too highly of what we can know for sure. So, Derrida and deconstruction teaches humbleness, a humbleness that stems from the fact that we never can rest assured that we are correct and righteous. That is the moral imperative of deconstruction. It is a constant reminder that we cannot know. Its center is therefore emptiness.

There is no room, or use, for supplications in a deconstructionist religiosity. The *Risale-i Nur* on the contrary is born from a firm contact with God, the All-Wise and All-Knowing. Where Derrida sees a faint and unreachable dream, Said Nursi sees an All-Powerful Maker and Sustainer. On that ontological level they are incompatible. In the discussions at the symposium I had difficulties in explaining what I was after and probably came through as odd to many of the religious participants. I still think that there is a kind of connection, as I tried to describe.

Deconstruction is about morality and justice. It is a morality in line with the phrases *Allahu Akbar* and *Deus semper Major*—God is the Greatest. But deconstruction says rather that reason is always smaller: not describing, not knowing that which compared to it is smaller. It might be seen as somewhat affiliated with Ismaili thought as expressed in the *Rasail Ikhwan as-Safa*, or negative theology taken to its very extreme. From that, it follows that there are fields of morality connected to classical ethical and religious virtues that it has little to say about. In a *hadith* recorded in *Sahih al-Bukhari* (8:477) Prophet Muhammad said, "He who remains patient, God will bestow patience upon him, and he who is satisfied with what he has, God will make him self-sufficient. And there is no gift better and vast (you may be given) than patience." Patience is a central virtue for all the Abrahamic faith traditions, but it might be even more important in Islam. On patience (*sabr*) Said Nursi wrote:

> [H]uman advances and the attainments of civilization, which are to be observed, have been made subject to him [man] not through his attracting them or conquering them or through combat, but due to his weakness. He has been assisted because of his impotence. They have been bestowed on him due to his indigence. He has been inspired with them due to his ignorance. They have been given him due to his need. And the reason for his domination is not strength and the power of knowledge, but the compassion and clemency of the Sustainer and Divine mercy and wisdom: they have subjugated things to him.[65]

The All-Compassionate is one of the central Divine Names in the *Risale-i Nur*. It is He Who sits at the supreme tribunal. But the workings of the All-Compassionate are beyond even the hopes of Derrida who only operates on the level of human reason.

There are some similarities in the experiences from the margins of modernity that Derrida and Said Nursi have, and there are similarities in their critiques of one dimensional positivism and an overconfident assurance that human reason alone can govern the world. From a post-structuralist perspective, religion can be seen as encompassing a reasonable humbleness in front of the incalculability of existence. A Nur perspective could find support for the need of religious morality to con-

---

[65] Said Nursi, *The Words*, 337.

trol the scientific advances of modernity in Derrida's writings. Both per-spectives argue that true justice is beyond the reach of human reason. But their respective strategies and aims should not be subsumed with-in each other.

There are also unbridgeable differences especially regarding the role of a Creator, and of Revelation. How big a difference is it to be humble before an All-Mighty Creator, and being humble in relation to a funda-mentally inaccessible complexity? Even if I were not sure about the details of my argument, I still hold on to the overall claim. The differenc-es between Derrida and Nursi on the subject of true justice are no big-ger than the differences between Derrida and the students of material-istic philosophy Nursi is so critical of.

We should not continue to divide the debate along the lines of Islam and Western philosophy.

It only hides more than it shows.

The presentations at these Said Nursi conferences are simultaneous-ly translated between Turkish, Arabic and English. The largest common language between the participants was Arabic. I belonged to the minor-ity that had no knowledge of Arabic. This was instructive enough to make it worth the visit: For several days I was one of those that did not know the central common language, one that did not know the common Islam-ic tradition with its canon of writers, ideas and concepts as well most others in attendance, one who did not share the dominant faith. This happens all too seldom to a European male like me.

Most speakers started their presentation with the *basmala*—"In the Name of God, the All-Merciful, the All-Compassionate" (*Bismillahir-Rahmanir-Rahim*). For me this is an opening into another world, a world where over time I have made more and more friends and acquaintanc-es and also have learned to feel more and more at home; as a marginal figure, odd but accepted. I, who so often am one of the ordinary, nor-mal guys, need these experiences. Hopefully they can make me more humble as to the reach and relevance of my frame of reference. At least, this is one of the aims of my attendance there, one of the reasons for writing this book. Sure, I want to say something new and clever about Turkish Islam, but it is more important that I manage to show that it is a possible and respectable perspective on the world; that I do not write as if secular critics, like me, are more open and unbiased than religious thinkers. Late one night at the conference, I came to sit with a Bosnian couple, Mrs. and Mr. Mahmutćehajić, and a Bulgarian, Mr. Todorov, and was drawn into a conversation on the latter's work on a Bulgarian translation of the Qur'an. The conversation hinged on the Surah al-Fatiha, the opening chapter of the Qur'an. Rusmir Mahmutćehajić suggested examples from some old Bosnian translations. How is it possible to interpret and form the semantic flow of the Arabic text? Mahmutćehajić argued passionately for viewing the Qur'an as a coherent semantic whole, a phonetic world to enter and stay inside. Rather than reading and trying to interpret the words of God, reading the Qur'an is a way to become enclosed in the speech of God. To him, the Qur'an is still primarily recited, and he held that you can tell the difference between interpreters who have the Qur'an in their memory and recite the verses aloud as they interpret them, and modern exegetes who sit with silent pages in front of them when they work. Even if this is a revelation addressing reason, the message and experience become truncated if you do not let forth the phonetic world of the Qur'an. Mahmutćehajić did not talk about reading the Qur'an, he talked about spending time with it, being in the Qur'an. It is much more than a mere text or message; it is a meditative mental location, a surface from which contact with God can be made.

How on earth is it possible to maintain all the intricate semantic conceptual ties of the Qur'anic Arabic in such a language so different as Bulgarian? How can you at least try to describe what is lost when the text is rendered in another language? These questions are important for all of us who read texts in translations. The sincerity and meticulousness that these experienced persons showed in their reflections on these questions moved me deeply. Then and there I felt that such an approach to a text generates wisdom in itself, almost without regard to what the text itself is.

A central aspect of being in the presence of the Qur'an, or any other holy text, is that you are confronted with difficult passages. Instead of simply dismissing such passages as anachronistic, the revelation requires that we confront them and find ways of getting around them without denial. Wisdom also springs from this fervent wrestling with the difficult.

Then again: from a historical perspective it is odd to think about texts as a path to human wisdom. Texts are a fairly new and rare feature of human experience. As I think about it, I would be reluctant to claim that only those who have been able to read have developed wisdom. Texts are just as often a hindrance to wisdom, more of a source for superciliousness and fundamentalism. Plato distrusted writing, precisely because it fixes meaning and moves it to contexts different from those where it was formulated and could be thoroughly understood. Often, it leads us incorrectly to reason along an either-or line. My grandfather, Sten Falk, one of my primary role models in my life, did not have his wisdom from books. He was a farmer, firmly rooted in that tradition, whose attitude to life came from the respectful and interested interplay with fellow humans, animals and nature. Wisdom can surely be gained from different paths. The sincere and committed engagement with a text is one way. One result of a long reflective engagement with the text seems to be the realization that the text gives different answers depending on what one brings to the reading. A fundamentalist is no meditative, open re-reader, rather an effective learner of unambiguous certainties. Once again we see the importance of reflection.

In Islamic guidance, in the giving of advice, in *fatwas*, the oral form has been preserved up to the present time. Both Said Nursi and Gülen break with this form. A *fatwa* has traditionally been articulated in response to a specific question from a specific person, possibly from a group. The answer, the *fatwa*, is given to the one who came with the question. It is possible, even probable, that someone else asking the same question would get a different answer. The right and faithful action in a given situation differs according to the actor. Some of us are cautious and need to be spurred; in some, the reckless needs to be rectified—in accordance with sound Aristotelian ethics. Most often we cannot do the right thing. The right thing is the mean between to extremes. To reach that place we should strive towards the extreme that is furthest from our own temperament. Therefore two persons facing the same situation can get differing advice, differing *fatwas*.

Chapter 10

Writing about Islam

At the University of Gothenburg I had a colleague who became very important to the direction of my future work. From the room next door I had gotten used to hearing a constant stream of music, anything from bebop to Tibetan throat singing. The only sure thing was that it was never quiet. The man responsible for the selection of music was science theoretician Jan Bärmark.

He always had his door welcomingly open and took time to chat if I stuck my head in. Bärmark is a Buddhist who spent his research days studying Tibetan Buddhist medicine, from a theory of science perspective. After I came back from my İstanbul trip I sat more and more frequently on his couch and discussed how it would be possible to write about Islam without becoming yet another in a line of Orientalists who project their own wishes on the religion and remain confident in their ability to explain the world from a secure place, taken for granted as a Western male.

Luckily this was a question that Bärmark had pondered for many years and even formulated his own little research field around. He called it anthropology of knowledge. I found the name rather mossy and it took some time before I started to realize that I had a lot to learn from it. Together with Jan, I was already involved in teaching a course he said was about the anthropology of knowledge, but I mainly focused on Islam and the relation between Islam and science.

Gradually I had more and more thoughts about if and how the anthropology of knowledge could help me find a way to write about Turkish Islam that I could be content with.

According to Bärmark, we are involved in the anthropology of knowledge when:

> We are having a dialogue with another culture in order to learn something, to widen the border of our own culture's conceptions of knowledge, reason and truth. We might also dialogue with the other culture to deconstruct its conceptions, to see what they say and cannot say about reality.[66]

It seemed very close to what I wanted to do. Despite the humble wish to learn from the other culture, there is in what he says a belief in a firm difference between us and them. Even if we learn much about the other, it is still someone else's tradition, and one remains a stranger. It bothered me.

The culture, or cultures, we grow up with are probably in some respect always "our own." Even if we distance ourselves from our background, it will always remain part of what formed us, and we know it. I agree with that. But this doesn't have to mean that another culture cannot also become truly and fully one's own, does it? That one cannot belong to two or more communities?

How can we talk about cultures as separate entities where there is a clear line saying what is mine and what belongs to someone else? Maj-Lis Follér also discussed the possibilities of the anthropology of knowledge. I learned a lot from her, when I worked with her on a previous research project. In her views on the anthropology of knowledge, there was the same distinction between one's own culture and the other culture. Follér's examples came mainly from her field work with the Chipibo-Conibo in Peru.[67] It is not so difficult to see a clear difference between Chipibo-Conibo culture and Swedish culture. But, Maj-Lis is not only Swedish, and an individual Chipibo-Conibo person is not just a representative of the Chipibo-Conibo. When it comes to concrete indi-

---

[66] Jan Bärmark, "Att tänka genom kulturer: Om kunskap, förnuft och kultur" in *Vest* 2, (1992) 43.

[67] Maj-Lis Follér, "Reflektioner över ett kulturmöte: fältarbetet som kontext" in *Vest* 2, (1992) . Jan Bärmark and Maj-Lis Follér, "Förståelsen av det främmande" in *Tvärsnitt*, 4 (1991).

viduals it is always more complicated. I know that Maj-Lis speaks Spanish, that she has lived in South America, that she has children with a Greek man born in Turkey, that her grandchildren are Australian. She thus belongs to more "we's" than a narrow Swedish one.

Chipibo-Conibo is a name denoting a group comprised of different persons. One common characteristic is that they speak a language that Maj-Lis does not. Some of them also speak Spanish, though. They have lived all their lives in Peru, a state formed by Spanish colonialism. You could say that Peru is a modern state, like Sweden. There would thus seem to be some similarities between some Chipibo-Conibo people and a specific Swede called Maj-Lis Follér, with similar experiences and ties to traditions that make it harder to say exactly where the culture of one ends and the other's culture starts.

Borders between Cultures?

Where can you find the demarcation line between Turkish and Swedish culture? Is there also a difference between Turkish culture and Muslim culture? If so, is there also a difference between Swedish and European culture? In the media, the border between Christian and Muslim culture is often portrayed as straight and secure, even if they are both theistic, Abrahamic religions. Both Islam and Christianity also partly rest on the foundations of the Classical Greek philosophical heritage. As a historian of ideas I have worked to show that they are both Aristotelian traditions (even if Gülen would not express himself in that manner).

The claimed difference is difficult to pinpoint. How then can we talk about thinking through another culture (Islam) to understand our own (Swedish, Western)? It seems very difficult to draw a line where one culture ends and the other commences. And I was reluctant to do so for reasons that were not only theoretical. I couldn't accept such a difference. It was an emotional thing, it made me annoyed.

If you construe the scale Swedish-European-Turkish-Muslim it seems obvious that Swedish and Muslim are on separate ends, clearly separated. Still, Turkish is close to European, for in Turkish nationalism it is central to be both modern and European. Where in the series shall we place Christianity? It seems as if we must have another set to see religious-cultural differences. And then we return to the difficulties with the possible differences within the theistic Hellenic-Abrahamic religions.

As long as we are actually in the borderlands, it is hard to see where the border is located. It is much more obvious on the abstract map. This might be one of the explanations as to why we tend to study the typical forms of a culture, and avoid the turbid border thinking that in fact is much more common. To retain the belief in distinct cultural differences one has to stick to what is typical in each culture, even if it means that this difference is then construed to fit the cartographic purposes of one's study, rather than following from the look of the terrain.

I cannot understand in what way Voltaire, for example, who is counted as belonging to my tradition and culture, should in any qualitative way be closer to me than Gülen (whom I have read more often and more carefully than I have Voltaire). It is true that Voltaire's legacy has been present in the forming of the Swedish society I grew up and live in. But this also goes for the Turkish society that Gülen has grown up and worked in.

I have never lived in France, and I have never been close to experiencing how life was lived there, or at home in Sweden, in the 18th century. I have no experience of being noble and rich. I have spent quite some time in Turkey, though, and I find it much easier to recognize the simple country life that Gülen was formed by. Even if Gülen is of a different generation than I am, I have seen parts of the modernity his thinking goes against. Both of us have taken care of cows and sheep. I find it much harder to imagine life in the fancy Parisian 18th century circumstances of Voltaire.

What Bärmark was getting at was rather that there is a vital difference between someone who is fully within a tradition, and only in that one, like a Tibetan monk brought up in Tibet, and someone who had come to feel at home in the two or more traditions, like the Swedish philosopher of science and Buddhist Jan Bärmark. Through 30 years of studies of Tibetan Buddhism he has changed, but not into someone completely different, as he writes in his book *The Healing Buddha*: "We

cannot and shall not free ourselves of our Western anchorage."[68] Bärmark does not aim at being a modest witness and intermediary to Tibetan Buddhism and medicine. His texts are not conveying facts about
Buddhism for the sake of increased knowledge; the aim is rather to
produce insights so that we in the end can understand ourselves better. This gives nerve to the presentation, a nerve that also springs from
an honest self-disclosure that is still far from self-centered. The Western schooling of Bärmark is put in relation to Tibetan Buddhism.

Bärmark is a role model for me, and without his support and encour-
agement I would not have embarked on writing this book. Along the
way I have come to understand that these types of discussions are also
to be found in the field of religious studies. This is a common thing.
Scholarly fields live largely unaffected by each other and develop within their own parameters. There is so much written that it is almost
impossible for anyone to have an overview of what goes on in all the
other fields. A few thinkers will be made into icons of their time and thus
affect many different fields; apart from these large currents, a more mundane development of arguments and methods is taking place in internal journals and conferences. I have tried to get an understanding of the
religious studies discussions in conversations with religion scholars I
have met at conferences on Gülen and Turkish Islam, and via some religious studies journals. One thing I have noticed in these discussions is
the different ways in which the demand for scholarly objectivity is meted
out. It seems rather mundane that for example economists prescribe
the economic theory they study, that historians of philosophy like the
philosopher they have chosen to specialize in and can write about his
positive role in understanding contemporary society. In religious studies most who write about Christianity and Judaism also identify with
these traditions, if in different and often critical ways. In many subject
areas, most textbooks have an insider's perspective. When it comes to
Islam the opposite is true, and it is very unusual to find an insider's voice,
so unusual that if we hear one it comes forth as biased and uncritical.[69]

---

[68] Jan Bärmark, *Den läkande Buddha*, (Stockholm: Carlsson, 2007) 175.
[69] Amir Hussain, "Teaching Insidie-Out: On Teaching Islam" in *Method and Theory in
the Study of Religion,* vol 17 (2005).

What difference does it make? Here the religious studies research crosses a broader strand of anthropological discussions that Barbara Tedlock has described as the turn from participant observation to the observation of participation. It has lead anthropologists to develop a way of writing that through focusing on the participants and the processes in ethnographic dialogue becomes a way of telling about oneself as well as the other.[70]

The religious anthropologist Faydra Shapiro has given a very personal description of her relation to the vague Jewish heritage of her US upbringing, and the gradual development of a more engaged relation to her Jewish identity under a period of field work on Judaism in Israel. While talking to a friend, she suddenly realized that she had started considering whether or not her own way of expressing Jewishness was good for the Jews. She interpreted this as if the love of the tradition had changed her, in a surprising and initially unsettling way. She used to welcome any individual expression of Judaism, but found herself to be more and more preoccupied with the group and the traditional, imagined communities she felt a growing personal responsibility for.[71]

My history is different. The anthropological idea of participation always has to do with being among people. I think Bärmark and I share a difference from this idea of participation because we spend more time with texts than with representatives of a culture. What I am after is quite simple: honesty. Nothing should be held back, I think. Still, I recognize myself when Shapiro explains how a deepened love of the object under study leads to a changed understanding and a stronger sense of responsibility towards traditions. This sense of responsibility and respect can only grow in relation to real people, I think. Texts might give food for thought, but a solitary reading of text will be too intellectual. It is eventually about improving our relations to each other as citizens of the world, and to the world itself. To find a sense of belonging

---

[70] Barbara Tedlock, "From Participant Observation to the Observation of Participation: The Emergence of Narrative Ethnography," *Journal of Anthropological Research* 47, no.1 (1991).

[71] Faydra Shapiro, "Autobiography and Ethnography: Falling in Love with the Inner Other," *Method and Theory in the Study of Religion* 15 (2003): 198.

in, and understanding of, our global future I think it is vital to develop some kind of dual vision, or border thinking. What other tradition we choose to go into dialogue with is arbitrary, even if I have my reasons to think that it is especially important that more people improve their relationship with Islam, and a more nuanced image of Turkey.

Chapter 11

A Meeting at the Journalists
and Writers Foundation

I headed to the Journalists and Writers Foundation (JWF) for a lunch meeting. At that time, their office was less than a ten-minute walk from Taksim square, on the fifth and sixth floor of a building with a view facing the inner part of the Golden Horn. Far away on the other side of the water you could see Eyüp, the district where the Prophet's Companion Abu Ayub al-Ansari is buried. The mosque there is one of the holiest and most important places in Islam.

In the reception at JWF, I was greeted by Fatma; she spoke American English and did not wear a headscarf. The JWF was founded in 1994 on Gülen's initiative. When I had contacted the official Gülen web page saying I was coming to İstanbul and wanted to meet someone to ask some questions about Gülen and have the opportunity to buy his books, I had gotten the answer that the "friends" at JWF would be glad to receive me and help me.

JWF organizes sympathizers of Gülen from the media and academic circles. They have initiated and host the Abant Platform which is of great importance for the openness of Turkish public debate, as well as a range of other dialogue activities. They also receive many guests and inform them about Gülen, Said Nursi and the current situation in Turkey. Central to their activities is religious dialogue and the spreading of information to show the Turkish public sphere that a religious way of life does not constitute any threat to democracy or human rights.

I came to JWF at the same time as two other parties, two women from the US, and a British Protestant priest and his wife. Cemal Uşşak received us in a room with sofas along all four walls. We sat down in a corner and were offered tea or coffee. We introduced ourselves and explained why we were there. Cemal gave some information on the JWF and showed a pop video with the Kurdish singer Mahsun Kırmızıgül, who had written a song for the big meeting of representatives of all the Abrahamic religions in Turkey, held in Urfa, in south-east Turkey, Abraham's claimed city of birth.

In the song Orthodox bells are mixed with Jewish horns, Catholic choir singing and the Muslim call to Prayer in a florid and powerful refrain called "Not One of Us." Those who take inspiration from things other than love and solidarity with the Prophets Musa (Moses), Isa (Jesus) or Muhammad, and preach intolerance in their names are not one of us, Kırmızıgül is singing, all dressed in white on the stage in Urfa.

Kırmızıgül is an interesting person. He became popular in the late 1990s as a typical Arabesque singer with a powerful Kurdish way of singing, a heavy mustache and few signs of urbanity. The arabesque is a popular kind of music, often sung by macho men, which gathers large crowds.[72] Kırmızıgül's debut album garnered record sales. Musically he is close to that tradition, even if he writes his own songs with lyrics about his Kurdish background, about human rights, religious tolerance, and of course about love. He has also written and directed several well received films, among them *Five Minarets in New York*.

In the video from Urfa the Jewish chief rabbi, the Syrian-Orthodox archbishop, the Greek-Orthodox patriarch, the Catholic envoy to İstanbul, and a number of other religious leaders stood side by side. After we had watched the film we conversed for a while. What we spoke about had nothing to do with what knowledge of Islam, or Said Nursi, or Gülen, but about what insights we had reached. I was unaccustomed to this and felt inconvenienced by this situation, which felt more like Pentecostal testimony than scholarly disputation. I hadn't come there to meet these other people nor to engage in any dialogue. I had only a few hours

---

[72] A fantastic book about Turkish society through the lens of arabesque music is Martin Stokes, *The Arabesk Debate: Music and Musicians in Modern Turkey* (Oxford: Clarendon Press, 1992).

and I wanted to have as much information as possible, get my material and be off back to Gothenburg with it.

One of the American women told us about her conversion to Islam four or five years ago. She had up till then been a practicing Catholic. When she came in contact with the Qur'an, she immediately felt that she had met a purer and clearer word of God. Through a process that included a divorce she turned to Islam. Still, she said, that it did not mean any radical change in her life. It was just a slight reformulation of her life's basis. The first years she continued using the Catholic prayers she had prayed since childhood in the Muslim Daily Prayers, and only a year ago had she learnt the Qur'anic prayers in Arabic and started to use them. She had not taken any Muslim name and was very clearly American with her polite and positive appearance.

I was moved by her story, even if I was narrowly focused on getting answers to my questions about Gülen and wasn't prepared to engage in any polite conversation with people I would only meet for a few hours. It took me quite a while to realize that Cemal and Fatma had answered my questions with practice rather than information. I had more insight than knowledge from my visit. I was disappointed, but slowly I have started to get an understanding for what they are engaged in. I still find it hard, though.

I am trained in a critical tradition, and as political theorist Wendy Brown has argued the concept of critique is closely tied to a wish to expose the mystifications and illusions of religion and idealism. The tradition goes from Voltaire, Diderot, Kant and Marx, via Nietzsche, Freud and the Frankfurt school, and on to Foucault, Habermas and Cultural Studies. At least in Swedish humanities this is seen as "our" tradition.

I have worked as a university lecturer in Cultural Studies and the History of Ideas, teaching class after class inscribing this genealogy of critical humanistic thinking. I still identify with this perspective. I am a political person, and my ideological foundation is of the left, seeing the social world as inherently formed by antagonism. With this critical identity goes a certain cynicism. Everything can be revealed for the ideological interests it carries, and this often leads to a detached relation to the world. My pride is that I can see through any idealistic claim. It is still hard for me to take on the challenge from religious friends, from Hizmet or any other religious group: leave this secure cynicism behind, engage, and stand by a claim to try to do good. This has probably had the strongest impact on me. I now want to be more loving, unconcerned with having the right references and using hip concepts to impress; just learn to stand by the wish to be a better man, even if it is uncool. I often fail, in both aspects.

Cemal Uşşak was an understated person, with a mild expression, inviting eyes and a well-kept mustache. He was also one of the few persons I have met in all of the different Nur circles I have come in contact with. It might easily look as if those engaged in Nur are a very peculiar group, reading only their own masters and talking about their Islam. Cemal is a good example of how many people most often talk about Islam as such, and only infrequently quote or refer to Said Nursi or Gülen. Cemal filled his conversation with quotes from the Qur'an, always in Arabic. If Fatma was present he translated into Turkish, and she into English. When she was not there, Cemal emphasized that his English could only give a scent of the deeper meaning of the Qur'anic Arabic.

During that meeting, he talked about what Islam says and what it inspires him to do, not about what Said Nursi or Gülen say. Instead he became slightly awkward when I fired my questions about Gülen at him, about the editing of his books, about their distribution channels. On the top floor we were treated to lunch, assorted mezes with Cola Turka to drink.

A few weeks after I had been in İstanbul and met the Nur people, I got an e-mail from a man in Gothenburg called Muammer Kadal. He would like to meet me, he writes. We make an appointment to meet at my office in the university. It turns out that Muammer has worked as a journalist together with Cemal. Now he is engaged in Gülen-inspired activities in Sweden and wants to invite me to a program on the theme of Compassion which will be held on Prophet Muhammad's birthday (*mevlid*).

I find this typical of how the movement works. It has happened to me several times since. People in Sweden whom I have never met have contacted me with greetings from Hizmet friends from other parts of the world and informed me about events. This is not a structured organization, it is rather a network held together by bonds of friendship and common interests that are activated when someone sees the possibility of doing something. An important hub has been the newspaper *Zaman*. The journalists and correspondents at *Zaman* are knowledgeable about Gülen-inspired activities in different parts of the world. They distribute this information in the different local editions of *Zaman*, and also in informal meetings. But there are no bosses in the movement, no formal lines of command. It is a very modern network built on mutual and equal interests, even if there are also structured ways of cooperating.[73] I have met several persons who say that the more egalitarian, Hizmet way of deciding on activities has trained them to challenge the authoritarianism of their Turkish upbringing and education. There is a clear spirit of entrepreneurship in the movement, and the people involved are good at contacting the friends of friends who might have something to teach about successful events they have organized in their city.

A number of Turkish students with leftist sympathies I have met are mainly hesitant towards Hizmet because of the neoliberal ideals of the movement. It is not Hizmet's Muslimness that is seen as a problem; they say that Hizmet is not engaging with the radical anti-capitalistic ethos of Islam. In contrast to their parents in the secular upper middle class, these students are interested in affirming some sort of Muslim identity, but have difficulties finding any broader Sunni movement in Turkey expressing the social message of Islam while also being open towards another perspective on gender, sexuality, normativity and capitalism.

Time to Start!

I think this will work. It is possible to write a more personal, existentially grounded representation opening towards a dialogical way of thinking. It might even be possible to aim for insights.

---

[73] For more on organizational issues see Joshua D. Hendrick, *Gülen: The Ambiguous Politics of Market Islam in Turkey and the World* (New York: New York University Press, 2013).

Via Muammer I had gotten to meet more people in my home town who were inspired by Gülen's preaching, and for every visit in Turkey I met more participants of the movement and I felt I started to understand a few things.

I had written a few articles on Islamic philosophy. There I could always lean on being a historian of ideas, and even if it was somewhat odd to write about Muslim philosophers everyone could see that the differences between medieval Islamic and Christian philosophy was very small. If my field could harbor this, it could probably also harbor the other.

To stay on the safe side I started working on Gülen's understanding of science. Did Gülen have a theory of science? Did he relate to the theoreticians who were important in the Western academic discussions? Here I found questions where I could rest on my expertise and my academic legitimacy. The step towards a freer way of writing did not become as great as I had hoped for.

Chapter 12

Religion and Science—Faith and Knowledge

I slam of the Turkish type that Gülen represents carries different traits than for example Arabic, Malaysian or Indian Islam. Even if Turkish Islam has always had a split relationship with the modern state, they share points of departure which means that Gülen's representation of Islam differ from Turkish Islam of the 17th and 18th centuries.

During the end of the 19th century, a number of Muslim scholars argued that there was no contradiction between Modern-Western science and the teachings of the Qur'an. An early representative was the Indian scholar Sayyid Ahmad Khan (d. 1898). He held that nothing in the Qur'an contradicted modern scientific knowledge, or the natural laws formulated by science. If there seemed to be contradictions between the content of a verse of the Qur'an and Copernican astronomy—as many claim there is—we must, according to Khan, assume that the Qur'anic formulation was not meant as astronomical information but as a more metaphorical expression of something else. Similar discussions were at the same time conducted within Christianity on the Bible.

A genre of Qur'anic exegesis called *tefsir ilmi* (the science of Qur'anic exegesis) was developed around the turn of the 19th century, focused in Egypt. Within this field a scholar such as Ghulam Ahmad Pervez of India claimed that he found Darwin's theory of evolution expressed in the Qur'an.[74]

[74] Stefan Wild, "Political Interpretations of the Qur'an" in Jane Dammen McAuliffe (ed.), *The Cambridge Companion to the Qur'an* (Cambridge: Cambridge University

Bediüzzaman Said Nursi saw late technical innovations like railroads and radio mentioned in the Qur'an. The Qur'an contains the knowledge of all times, and every time reveals new layers of meaning in the divine revelation. The French convert Maurice Bucaille became an important and widely spread representative of the efforts to find scientific theories in the Qur'an during the late 20th century. In Turkey, Bucaille has had an impact and I have met a fair number of people in Nur circles who argue along the lines of this tradition. Ali Ünal, one of the main translators of Gülen's work into English, and the writer of a translation and commentary of the Qur'an in modern English, once translated Bucaille into Turkish.

Nowadays the main representative of this line of thought in Turkey is Harun Yahya. Harun Yahya is a pen name under which over 200 books have been published, and translated into over 40 languages. The real Harun Yahya is called Adnan Oktar, a grandiose figure often posing in white suits. The work of Harun Yahya is the product of a whole group of writers. One of the most well-known writers publishing under the name used to be the journalist Mustafa Akyol. He now writes for the English language daily *Hürriyet Daily News* and has won international acclaim for his book *Islam without Extremes: A Muslim Case for Liberty*. Akyol has been involved in the intelligent design movement in the US and among other things testified in favor of introducing intelligent design in the famous Kansas evolution hearings. Without going into details, it is worth mentioning that Akyol and most Muslims do not have any argument against the adaptation of species to changing environments, nor with the earth being billions of years old. The key question is whether life is a result of random evolution, or the design of God, and if there is any scientific evidence supporting either view.

Today, Akyol mainly writes about the compatibility of Islam and liberalism and also can be found in Hizmet settings, even if the people I know would not count him as one of the movement. (He considers himself as "sympathetic outsider".)

Press, 2006).

Harun Yahya, whoever has written his books, does not find any signs of evolution theory in the Qur'an; he is instead in liaison with the ID-movement in the US. Among his innumerable publications trying to refute Darwinism we find the huge *Atlas of Creation,* in many heavy volumes filled with colorful images. Harun Yahya's supposed counter-evidence against evolution all follows the same pattern. It can also be seen in a number of short films on his web page www.harunyahya.com. They often look like this: One film shows a camel, with a voiceover speaking about how well adapted it is to live in the harsh desert conditions. The anatomy of the camel is described in careful detail. The film closes with a quote from the Qur'an and a conclusion that it hardly can be a coincidence that the camel can survive in its habitat. There has to be a Creator. This classical *argument from design* is repeated over and over again by Harun Yahya, with many images taken from the internet without respect for copyrights.

An advantage Muslim critics of evolution have over Christians is that the Qur'anic description of creation is less detailed than the Biblical one. Islam has never been tied to the short span of time the Christians have had to work with. Fossils millions of years old are no problem; the question is whether they can show that life has developed randomly and without purpose. Harun Yahya's argument is most often crude and simplistic.[75] Mustafa Akyol on the other hand has gone on to say that "evolution is a solid fact." He can also acknowledge Darwin's work as giving insights into mechanisms of the evolutionary process. The dividing line is whether these mechanisms function randomly and purposelessly, and if this is an unproven axiom in science, or the valid result of scientific inquiry.

I will not spend time mocking Harun Yahya. His movement should not be laughed at. It has huge resources and many readers. Many of the books in his name are worth reading and follow the wide path of traditional Islam, especially those on the Qur'an and the fundamentals of the Muslim faith. In almost every book there can be found a few anti-

[75] Anne Ross Solberg, *The Mahdi Wears Armani: The Harun Yahya Enterprise* (Stockholm: Södertörn University Press) 2013.

Darwinistic sentences. Harun Yahya also speaks warmly about dialogue and tolerance, even if his world view tends to be painted in black and white and portrays freemasons, Zionists, and Darwinists as Satanic, responsible for all evil on earth. Harun Yahya has also given room to Holocaust deniers and other shady revisionists.

Fethullah Gülen has been critical of the tradition that tries to find correspondences between today's scientific facts and verses of the Qur'an. "The great volume of articles and books produced in this vein in recent times will be open to ridicule in the future."[76]

The wisdom of the Qur'an does not need any external support, Gülen stresses. Trying to find such support means giving science priority; it is as if saying that the Qur'an needs to prove itself to science. We can never make the truth of the Qur'an and Hadith rely on being scientifically verified. Scientific findings are always incomplete and unrelated to the meaning and purpose of life taken as a whole. Scientific truth changes as the boundaries of human knowledge expand, says Gülen. Saying that the Qur'an expresses a particular scientific theory will cause great troubles in the long run. The short term gain of piggy-backing on the status of science will backfire and become a kiss of death in the longer perspective. It temporalizes the timeless message, and thus betrays it.

> What we must, and do, reject is that the truth of Qur'an and *hadith* should be made to depend on verification and confirmation by scientific data which are, as explained above, incomplete, disconnected from the meaning and purpose of life as a whole, and vulnerable to change as the borders of human ignorance change.[77]

Still, Gülen must be counted to the tradition of Qur'anic exegetes that take a sincere interest in modern science. Science is one of Gülen's prime interests. "A community's survival depends on idealism and good morals, as well as on being able to reach the necessary level in scientific and technological progress," says Gülen.[78] In all his work these

---

[76] Gülen, *Questions & Answers about Islam (Vol. 2),* (New Jersey: Tughra Books. 2010) 105.

[77] M. Fethullah Gülen, *The Essentials of the Islamic Faith*, (New Jersey: The Light. 2005) 233.

[78] Gülen, *Towards a Global Civilization*, 208.

two aspects have been fundamental. There is no tension between science and religion in his mind. The biggest mistake of modern history has been the misconception about such a contradiction. Western modernity parted with religion, the Muslim mainstream abandoned science. They both lost. Gülen's aspiration can be summarized as the will to reunite the two, and thus build a more tolerant and reasonable civilization.

During the last several hundred years science has evolved in the West. One of the primary methods of scientific investigation has been to examine the world in as small and demarcated slices as possible. The scientist pondering why, for example, people die of cancer should divide this problem into as many small parts as possible. Then these should be systematically investigated, part after part. Eventually the partial answers can be put together and a full explanation be given. Today many fields of science are specialized to an extent that no single researcher can survey the entireties any longer.

In many contexts, it is seen as unscientific to try to understand how it all fits together. Science's role as a servant for a good human life has been replaced by a reverence for science as an empty form, says Gülen. But science cannot give directions to its own endeavor. What questions and problems are worth exploring depend on whose ailments are prioritized; on what is seen as vital for a well-functioning society. These are ethical decisions, and modern science cannot produce its own ethics. Science is indispensable to a good society, but it cannot guide us in understanding what a good society is. This is an anormative question.

In order for science to free itself from its compartmentalized and materialistic conceptions of reality, Gülen says, it needs to be conducted within the spiritual and moral frame of Islam: "There is no reason to fear science. The danger does not lie with science and the founding of the new world it will usher in, but rather with ignorance and irresponsible scientists and others who exploit it for their own selfish interests."[79]

His discussions of science are often in tune with contemporary strands in the theory of science field gathered under the name of science and technology studies (STS). It is difficult to know whether his

[79] "Regrets About Science and Technology," *The Fountain*, January-March 1993.

arguments stem from readings of this field, or if he has come to similar conclusions from a different angle. He very strongly emphasizes that "none of the findings of scientific research are ever absolute." To support this claim he refers to the majority of scientists, without giving any references.

Thomas Kuhn described competing scientific theories as incommensurable if there is no common theoretical language that can be used to compare them. Since there is no place outside the scientific paradigms, different paradigms will judge each other's theories as flawed from their own perspectives. There is thus no absolute way to decide which theory is better. Gülen's argument about the impossibility of absolute scientific knowledge is in line with Kuhn's, but since there are no references in Gülen's texts, I cannot know if Gülen is influenced by Kuhnian perspectives. It is not considered necessary or desirable in traditional Islamic scholarship to refer to other scholars in the same way as in modern academia, as ideas and knowledge are held to belong to God, not to individuals. Gülen's standpoint on truth is also well in line with Islamic traditions.

Gülen's stance is also similar to the arguments for the Islamization of science developed by Ziauddin Sardar, especially during the 1970s and 1980s. The difference is that Sardar builds his arguments explicitly on Kuhn and other theorists of science. He also gives a lot of attention to the classical Islamic scientific tradition. According to Sardar, this is a strong and viable tradition within Islam worth connecting with and re-enlivening.[80] Gülen on the other hand talks about science as a modern creation of the West, if also having important predecessors in Islam.[81]

Sardar is critical of the reductionist ideals of science, a method that he claims had its logical endpoint with B.F. Skinner and the psychological behaviorists. The logic of reductionism reduces the sound scientific aim for objectivity to a perspective where everything in the world is seen merely as objects for the knowledge production of a scientific rea-

---

[80] Ziauddin Sardar, *Explorations in Islamic Science* (London: Mansell, 1989), and *Introducing Science* (London: Icon Books, 2002).

[81] Ergene, *Tradition Witnessing the Modern Age*, 63.

son. Only empirically observed data are allowed in the building of our understanding of the world. Objectivity becomes objectification. The terrible effects of Western excesses in colonialism, sexism, racism, and class hatred are reduced to effects of man's biological nature, Sardar writes.

I cannot help but think about a joke that Jan Bärmark, who also has aversions to Skinner, has told me: "The behaviorist after intercourse: was it pleasant for me too?"

Sardar also holds that scientific enterprises must be conducted within ethical boundaries, boundaries that contemporary science cannot set for itself. The Islamic scientific ideal is built on the concepts *tawhid* (unity), being a *khalifa* (responsibility for the creation of God) and *ibadat* (reverence and contemplation; humble worshipping or devotion to God). Within the framework set up by these concepts Islamic scientific knowledge can promote *adl* (social justice) and *istislah* (common interest).

Science depends on choices. And the choices made in Western science are not primarily for solving the problems of the third world. Instead of seeking cures for the common diseases that afflict large parts of the world's population, scientists put their energy and funds into transplantation research and in vitro fertilization. Even if research dollars were redirected towards common diseases like diarrhea and schistosomiasis, which are the biggest killers in Muslim countries, reductionist Western medicine could not solve these problems. It would require a holism that addresses the connections between medicine, irrigation, education, playgrounds for children, countryside development and agriculture. It would require an Islamic science, Sardar argued in the 80s.

Gülen has never argued that science needs to be Islamized. He sees Western science as indispensable for the creation of a just society and for a true understanding of creation. He is critical only of the tendency to see a contradiction between scientific knowledge, technical innovation and belief in God. Drawing materialistic conclusion based on science is incorrect, Gülen asserts. It is the disconnection of research into creation from the respect for the Creator that is the cause for contemporary brutality, pollution and exploitation of the world for selfish satisfaction. Science does not need to change in any fundamental way to become the positive force it could and should be. It only has to become more scientific and conscious about its own limitations. The values that should guide science are to be found in religion. Not exclusively in Islam, but also in the Christianity that guided modern science in its infancy.

The commitment to religious dialogue resonates in other parts of Gülen's thinking as well. Solutions are not to be found only within Islam. It should be noted that Sardar never meant for Islamic science to replace Western science; his claim was that every tradition must reclaim the specificity of its scientific heritage and produce knowledge specifically directed towards the needs of its own group. Sardar is promoting a pluralistic view of science and thus breaks with modernism's belief in objective knowledge.

Reflection and Science

"Encouraging people to engage in reflection focused upon a determined aim entails urging them to learn and use the methods of sciences that study how existence is manifested."[82] To know all the different parts of the Book of the Universe (*Kitab al-Manshur*), we need to study it empirically; to fully understand the meaning of the scientific knowledge we gain, we need to study the Qur'an, the written Book (*Kitab al-Mastur*).

But the means and methods (science) must never take precedence over the aim (love of God). Most of the time, science is a means to reach a whole number of Islamic aims, and it brings understanding and also helps us in our role as *khalifas* (vicegerents), in using and caring for the universe in a better way, since "loving something depends on knowing it well." Earlier, before the environmental and climatic crisis became everyday headlines, Gülen stressed that "We are to establish science and exploit natural resources by discovering the Divine laws of nature and reflecting on natural phenomena. However, while doing this, we should seek God's pleasure and practice Islam."[83]

Through reflection we can use the universe as a book, to study and learn from. But it is not something only to master and exploit, it is

---

[82] M. Fethullah Gülen, "Our World and its Inherently Exquisite Mystery," *The Fountain*, November-December (2009).
[83] Gülen, *Muhammad*, 194.

also a source for humbleness and respect. Here we can see a similar shift in Gülen as in most of society; at first, he talked without reservations about the positive aspects of man's mastery over nature, but now the need for respect is given more attention.

Gülen and Ramadan

On the relation between Islam and science there are many similarities between Fethullah Gülen and Tariq Ramadan. Ramadan is more academic, though, and more strongly emphasizes the need for reform. Gülen is more didactic, and traditional. They are both radical in the very literal sense of the word; the way to meet the needs of the present is to go back to the roots and revitalize the values of the Companions, values such as love of knowledge, openness to change, tolerance and free-thinking.

Both Gülen and Ramadan are Universalists; they do not want to develop or argue for a specific Muslim way to know, any specific Islamic knowledge, as Sardar does. "The methods, techniques, and scientific methodologies established to understand and analyze an object under study and realize how it functions are by no means inherently 'Islamic' [...] What is 'Islamic' are the ethics, the norms, and the goals that orient—and limit—the use of knowledge acquired," Ramadan writes.[84] This is very similar to Gülen's position. People should not fear science; it is the improper use of science that is the problem.

In Gülen's understanding, there is a clearer hierarchy between religion and science. "Religion guides the sciences, determines their real goal, and puts moral and universal human values before science as guides."[85] Also Ramadan stresses that science-in-and-for-itself is unstable, and might lead to catastrophic results. "For a believing conscience, what matters is not just to understand facts—although this in itself is essential—but also to understand the intents, meaning, and finality of the world's order and of the substance of the revealed message, where ultimately, the two revelations [the Universe and the Qur'an] meet."[86]

---

[84] Tariq Ramadan, *Radical Reform*, 128.
[85] Gülen, *Towards a Global Civilization*, 196.
[86] Tariq Ramadan, *Radical Reform*, 128.

Gülen talks about guiding science, Ramadan about giving it proper attention. The main argument of Ramadan's book *Radical Reform* is that there is a need to renegotiate the Islamic stance towards the sciences. "The Universe, the social and human context, has never been considered as a self-standing source of law and of its production. It is this status, this qualitative differentiation in authority—between the text and the context—that to my mind is a problem today."[87] This is radical indeed, and even though he does not mention Gülen I think Ramadan's critique also goes out to his position.

Gülen's main message is that there are ways of reconciliation between what is seen as opposing traditions; if both sides just understand their position more completely and realize their true ethos, we can build a universal civilization of love and tolerance. I think it is very important to see the different roles and genres of Gülen and Ramadan here. The differences we can see are partly related to the different dialogues they are involved in. As I said, Gülen is more didactic and is a spiritual guide; he aims for change and praxis. Ramadan is more academic; he is analytical and aims for critical thinking. But there is also the factual difference that Ramadan calls more for a reform of Islam. Gülen uses Islam to reform society, Ramadan thinks that the ever-changing societal context needs to reform Islam, emphasizing the distinction between the spheres of *mu'amalat* (social affairs), where reform is vital, and *aqidah* (the creed) and *ibadat* (worship), where the critique of *bid'ah* (innovation in religion) is applicable.

Ramadan, as his position is stated in *Radical Reform*, also sees science as more self-sufficient than Gülen. Ramadan accepts the argument that science and religion are two separate and equal entities that must be left to function according to their respective logic and axioms. No side has any right to interfere with the other. Gülen most often criticizes the use of science in modern Europe, but sometimes his critique also goes out to science as a practice. This is the interpretation Mehmet Enes Ergene gives when he writes that "science plunged into materialistic views and was forced to be one-dimensional—to ignore moral, religious,

---

[87] Ramadan, *Radical Reform*, 82.

and metaphysical concerns."[88] Science is necessary, but it should keep within the boundaries set by religion, Gülen thinks. Ramadan upholds the theory of complementarity and equality of science and religion. Science is free; the problem lies with the social interpretation and use of scientific results. Ramadan's main argument in *Radical Reform* is that scientists should be recognized as context scholars (*ulama al-waqi*), and be integrated on an equal plane in *fiqh* councils. Ramadan thus argues for a new synthesis of science and religion, Gülen talks about re-establishing a balance between science and religion, lost in both the West and in Islam.

In a broader (Islamic and/or Western) context I think the similarities of Gülen's and Ramadan's thinking about the role of knowledge are more striking than the differences.

Relation before Knowledge

In the words of Mehmet Enes Ergene: "Gülen clearly points to the old cosmological view that espoused the idea that the cause for the universe to exist was love and compassion." Ergene says that the cosmology preferred by Gülen "established a constant and causal relation among man, the universe, and God."[89]

To restate Gülen's criticism of materialist science: the major mistake is that it denies man's relation to the universe, and puts itself outside of what becomes a mere object. It denies the existence of relationships. In the words of the Archbishop emeritus of the Church of Sweden K. G. Hammar: "Faith is not primarily an alliance with a doctrine, or upholding certain theoretical truth claims. Faith is relation, and faith must always be personal".[90]

One etymology for the Latin word *religio* is that it means union, connectedness. I would like to interpret the critique of materialism as a

---

88 Mehmet Enes Ergene, *Tradition Witnessing the Modern Age: An Analysis of the Gülen Movement*, (New Jersey: Tughra Books, 2008) 76.
89 Ergene, *Tradition Witnessing the Modern Age*, 76.
90 Hammar, K G. and Lönnroth, Ami. *Jag har inte sanningen, jag söker den (I do not know the truth, I am seeking it)* (Stockholm: Ordfront, 2004) 45.

critique of science in the sense not so much of a denial of God but as of a denial of relationships, union, connectedness, responsibility. Maybe this is stretching the interpretation a little bit, but it has the advantage that it connects Gülen with interesting trends in contemporary Western thought otherwise quite unrelated to religion.

Gülen is in line with contemporary Western debates on science in two respects: on the contingency of scientific theories, and in the critique of the denial of relation. In the theory of science field this has been criticized as "the view from nowhere," where the observer becomes a "Master-of-all-I-survey." From a Jewish perspective, the philosopher Emanuelis Levinas criticized Western philosophy for putting ontology before ethics. The question that ought to come first in our meeting with the Other (the world around us) is not "How can this object be classified and explained?" but "What is my responsibility towards this subject?" The mistake is to transform thinking into theories about an indifferent world.[91]

Post-Cartesian philosophy has narrowed itself to discussions on what knowledge is and how it is produced. More and more critical thinking about modernity now argues that this concentration, although very productive in a techno-scientific respect, has lost many aspects critical for a sound understanding of what a good life might be. Questions not answerable via verifiable, empirical, physical observation were seen as metaphysical, and thus as meaningless and nonsensical. This was an important and valid limitation of the realm that can be known scientifically. The mistake was to say that questions were meaningless and unimportant just because they were impossible to falsify by reduction to physical observations.

This critique of positivist epistemology comes from different angles. Complexity theorist Stuart Kauffman states his critique from a biological point of view. He criticizes scientific reductionism from within.

> In physics, there are only happenings, only facts, only statements
> of fact about what 'is'. But we have seen that biology is not reduc-

---

[91] Levinas, Emmanuel, *Totalité et Infini: Essai sur l'Extériorité* (La Haye: Martinus Nijhoff, 1991).

ible to physics, nor is agency, an aspect of life, reducible to physics. With agency [...] values enter. Once this is true, meaning and 'ought' enter the universe. [...] But this agency-borne 'ought' is [...] not reducible to physics, and the language of bare facts, of what 'is'. [...] Values, meaning, doing, action, and 'ought' are real parts of the furniture of the universe. 'Ought' is central to much of human action and all our moral reasoning.[92]

We also find similar critique of reductionism and simplified objectivism from within the field of physics. In the fascinating book *Meeting the Universe Halfway* Karen Barad uses her expertise as a theoretical physicist and a feminist philosopher to argue for the entanglement of matter and meaning. The world does not consist of facts to be observed. The world is always coming into being and we always meet the universe halfway, that is—"we don't have the distances of space, time, and matter required to replicate 'what is;' in an important sense, we are already materially entangled across space and time with the diffractive apparatuses that iteratively rework the 'objects' that 'we' study."[93]

Neither Kauffman nor Barad departs from materialism. But their materialism seems to me to be something very different from the one that Gülen criticizes. They both hold that the world is constantly refigured by agency. And agency is everywhere, not only connected to intellect. Since the interconnectedness of agents is what shapes the world, there is no study of the world disconnected from ethics. "Ethics is about accounting for our part of the entangled webs we weave."[94] Our primary goal cannot be to know objects as accurately as possible; it must be to take responsibility for our meeting with the universe. "Since reason truly is an insufficient guide, we truly must reunite our humanity. And if so, we truly need to reinvent the sacred for ourselves to guide our lives [...]. At last, we must be fully responsible for ourselves, our lives,

---

[92] Kauffman, Stuart A. *Reinventing the Sacred: A New View of Science, Reason, and Religion,* (New York: Basic Books, 2008) 87.

[93] Barad, Karen. *Meeting the Universe Halfways: Quantum Physics and the Entanglement of Matter and Meaning,* (Durham, NC: Duke University Press, 2007) 384.

[94] Ibid., 384.

our actions, our values, our civilizations, the global civilization."[95] There is a dire need for reflection also for materialistic scientists, and Kauffman's and Barad's books can be described as sincere reflections on their scientific *and* existential knowledge.

Kaufmann is a theoretical biologist. His main area of research has been on the complexity of biological systems and organisms, proposing self-organization as an explanation, in addition to Darwinian natural selection. As seen, his work on complexity, emergence and evolution has led him to talk about re-inventing the sacred. I find his discussions on the relation between materialism and religion respectful and cautious about the reach of the limits to our knowledge.

Similarly I enjoy reading Gülen because of his principal openness and respect for knowledge produced in other fields, for example science. But there is one question where I feel this openness is abandoned. It is when Darwinism comes up. Gülen implies that Darwinism equals materialism, and thus with denial of God.[96]

According to the classical Islamic tradition, according to the *sharia*, denying God (apostasy) is a mortal sin. In many interpretations it has been advised that the punishment for the denier should be death. As mentioned in the beginning of the book, Gülen gives a creative reinterpretation of this edict. Noting that the death penalty for apostasy has never included women and children, he argues that what has been punished is really desertion. The edict is focused on treason. To leave Islam today, or to deny God, has nothing to do with treason, and thus does not fall under state legislation. It is still one of the most serious offenses against God. But since the offense is against God, God is the One Who shall impose the penalty. This will happen on the Day of Judgment. We cannot know God's intentions, and shall not judge others; a temporary denial of God might be part of a learning process for someone aimed to do great things for God. What if a finite and presumptuous person in this world of generation and corruption punishes what is according to God's plan merely a trial?

[95] Kauffman, *Reinventing the Sacred*, (New York: Basic Books, 2008), 282.

[96] Gülen, *Questions & Answers about Islam (Vol. 2)*, (New Jersey: Tughra Books. 2010) 117.

Still, it remains a fact that materialism and atheism are great sins, and that Darwinism preaches that there is no Creator. Gülen says that Darwinism is a scientific theory among others, in time it will be replaced by a better one. Gülen also criticizes Darwinism for being too certain of the truth of its claims. His argument that the theory of evolution is just a theory full of flaws, which leaves many things unexplained, is a rather standard one from religious critics. I find it hard to reconcile with his rhetorical and broad approval of the importance of scientific knowledge. I feel that when it comes to Darwinism, Gülen becomes defensive and categorical in a way I have not otherwise seen. For sure, it is a contentious issue. Still, I cannot interpret it in any other way than that Gülen resorts here to defense rather than argumentation. I find the same thing with the opposing side, with religious critics like Richard Dawkins. In a similar way he closes himself off to arguments and interprets simplistically any religious formulation with an understanding of God he claims to have refuted.

My Gothenburgian friend Selçuk Akti tells me I make too much of Gülen's defensiveness. What I have read is mainly sermons and answers to questions directed towards a broad Turkish public, a context where it is impossible to go into details. Most of these statements are also from the 1970s and 1980s. Some people I have talked to interprets Gülen's later silence on the subject as the beginning of a repositioning in relation to Darwinism. The relation between scientific theories and the message of the Qur'an must be interpreted in close collaboration with scientists, and in such contexts Gülen is more prone to take part in nuanced discussions on evolution, they say. And as far as I have been able to find, Gülen has never commented on intelligent design theory.

Defending Darwinism is often seen as the same as being a materialist opponent of the religious perspective. On the web site herkul.org, which presently is the main distributor of Gülen's message and sermons, Darwin figures only as a denier of God (even if only mentioned by writers other than Gülen). This makes me uncomfortable; I feel as if my sincerity is being questioned. I am certainly no Darwinist. As for most of the Hizmet representatives I have met I seldom think about Darwin. I know his work fairly well, having taught the History of Ideas in a university for ten years. I have read some of his works. Even if I can't make sense of the details, I am convinced by those who say that the broad evolutionary process as described by Darwin and developed and refined by later biology is one of the best scientific theories. Even Pope John Paul II stated, in 1996, that "new scientific knowledge has led us to the conclusion that the theory of evolution is no longer a mere hypothesis." This almost by definition means that a defense of Darwinism does not equal a denial of religion. The Catholic father George Coyne, SJ, has said:

> For those who believe modern science does say something to us about God, it provides a challenge, an enriching challenge, to traditional beliefs about God. God in his infinite freedom continuously creates a world which reflects that freedom at all levels of the evolutionary process to greater and greater complexity. God lets the world be what it will be in its continuous evolution. He does not intervene, but rather allows, participates, loves.[97]

I find it sad that evolution has come to be a battleground. There is no room for voices like Coyne's. The debate is heated and more concerned with proving the stupidity of the opponents than trying to understand them. Does evolution really have so much to do with the place of religion in society? For most of us, it is never an issue. In the secular debate Darwinism is sometimes treated as the first tenet of science. Anyone denying any detail of the theory of evolution has proven himself unmodern, and within the dichotomist logic of modernity this is taken to mean that he reject science as a whole.

I do think it is an interesting and important field where we can learn more about the relation between knowledge and faith. I do feel that intelligent design reduces the unfathomable to an uninteresting engineer. I am also certain that you can be a good Muslim, Christian, or Jew while supporting the theory of evolution. And I think, or hope, that reflecting on the relational character of knowledge can open a more bal-

---

[97] George V. Coyne, "Science Does Not Need God, or Does It? A Catholic Scientist Looks at Evolution," at Palm Beach Atlantic University in West Palm Beach, FL, Jan. 31, 2006. I thank SJ Thomas Michel for the transcript (in private archive).

anced dialogue between science and religion, beyond the mere comparison of scientific and scriptural facts and statements that has dominated for far too long.

At the start of the new semester, Faris Kaya reminded me of the workshop on resurrection and the afterlife in the *Risale-i Nur* that he had mentioned in our first telephone conversation. He asked if I wanted to attend. Of course I did, and I had a little research money to cover the cost.

The subject was quite foreign to me. I saw this as an advantage. It was time to let go and venture out on deep water where I could not hide behind my professional identity. I also felt I needed help to get on with Said Nursi's texts. His writings were opaque and I hadn't found a clear research question for my reading, as I had with Gülen. At the same time the *Risale-i Nur* attracted me, it was more of an adventure to read, and it was a text I could not read from a narrowly professional point of view. It spoke strongly about life choices; it made me think and reflect a lot and forced me out into other areas of the Islamic textual tradition. Above all it made me realize I had to find a much closer relationship to the Qur'an if I wanted to understand what Said Nursi was trying to tell me.

What could be better than the guidance of knowledgeable scholars? And of course I have never passed on an opportunity to come to İstanbul.

Chapter 13

A Meeting in İstanbul;
Some Beautiful Days in November

The sun shines through the exhaust vapor in central İstanbul. The last few days the temperature has been over 20 degrees Celsius, like Swedish summer, in November 2008. Lines of men fishing for anchovy fill the quays of the Golden Horn. Among the hundreds of men I have so far spotted two women with fishing poles. It is an image of Turkish society. However, there are more women in technical education and engineering here than there are in Sweden, a country often claiming to be the most equal of all.

I am staying in the Dragoman House at the Swedish Research Institute in the lower end of İstiklal Street, at Tünel. There is a well-stocked library and a few guest rooms here.

The first couple of days I visited three publishers and went into some of the bookseller districts to get an overview of the supply of Islamic literature—of English translations of Islamic material, as well as of the overall orientation. It is striking that most small book shops outside the main street (İstiklal) and the school book publishers in Cağaloğlu display religious literature. Many are even dominated by these kind of books; one often finds difficult texts by classical Sufi writers like Ibn Arabi, al-Ghazali and Imam Rabbani al-Sirhindi.

The most common of the classical texts are al-Ghazali's 11th century *Kimya-yi Sa'adat*. The original of this is a Persian summary of his grand *Ihya Ulum ad-Din*, Revival of the Religious Sciences. The summary extends over 1,000 pages and gives a comprehensive exposition of every aspect of a good Muslim life.

One seldom finds Said Nursi's or Gülen's books in book shops. Their texts are still distributed mainly through other channels. During the last couple of years Gülen has started to appear in İstiklal book shops, most frequently in the religiously oriented İnsan Books that opened a shop at Galatasaray in 2009. In the stalls outside many mosques you can often find CDs, VCDs and other digital products about Said Nursi and his texts. Gülen's message is widely distributed as recorded sermons on cassette, CD, video or via www.herkul.org.

Most books in the religious book stands are by Turkish authors; many are introductions and calendars covering important details of the religious practice. Along the copies of the Qur'an and commentaries on the Qur'an, prayer books are most frequent. They contain *dua*s, the free Islamic prayer that is more similar to the prayers practiced by Western Christians.

Not even in districts like Fatih or Eyüp, with reputations for being more radically religious, have I found any books by radical authors like Mawlana Mawdudi or Sayyid Qutb, who are so much in focus in contemporary Islamic studies.

A somewhat tentative conclusion is that the common Turkish reader outside of academia is not unlike the Evangelicals and Baptists that in Sweden used to be called "readers." They read as part of their religion. It is also possible to find support for the thesis that Turkish Islam in its absolute majority forms has another tone than that of the gruffer Arabic orthodoxy. The Nakşibendi perspective is strong.

Most book stalls also offer CDs and cassettes of Sufi music and recitations of the Qur'an. The use of digital materials is highly developed. In most stalls you can find Prayer instructions with very meticulous and pedagogic introductions to the correct execution of the Daily Prayers. These introductory materials could be seen promoting as a formalistic observance of the absolutely accurate execution of the Prayers as the straight path to Paradise, in line with the teachings of the Indian Tabligh Jamaat movement. They could also, and more probably, be interpreted as a sign showing that many contemporary Turkish Muslims are brought up without an intimate relationship with the religious tradition, and did not learn how to practice the tenets of the religion as children.

Window shopping in the book shops of central İstanbul can make one understand that Islam is an important part of Turkish identity, and that the international literature on Islam and modernity is not fully applicable in an analysis of the modern Turkish state. Islam is practiced and influences society in too many ways; preconceptions about universal tensions between Islam and modernity probably confuses more than they explain.

Window shopping also made me think about the role of the Alevites in Turkey. The Alevites are a tradition related to Shi'ism which constitutes as much as 20 percent of the population in Turkey. Instead of mosques, Alevites build prayer houses where men and women worship side by side. They do not abstain from alcohol and do not fast during the month of Ramadan. Politically they often defend Kemalist secularism, and are found on the left of the political spectrum. Alevite tradition is oral to a large extent.[98]

It is unusual to find books with obvious Alevite titles, or maybe it is just that I am not knowledgeable enough to spot them. Most music vendors sell Alevi music; in some stalls it is placed quite prominently. In the book stall outside mosques there is no Alevi music, though. Here and there in both religious and secular book shops one finds titles on freemasonic conspiracies. On the inner sleeves of all publications from Hakikat Publishing the editors ask the reader to be cautious against Christian missionaries, Jews, and freemasons who try to delude him. Freemasons in particular stand for dangerous secular materialism and hedonism. In order to counter their influence, the publishers work hard translating Islamic literature into English, German, French, Russian and a number of other languages. The energy, power and ability of these translating publishers are impressive. But I cannot help to wonder: Do they really reach anyone?

On Thursday morning I took the ferry over to Üsküdar on the Asian side of İstanbul. On the boat I had breakfast, a sesame pretzel and a glass of black tea. I was going to visit the Light Publishing. I had e-mailed them

---

[98] On alevism, see *Alevi Identity*, Tord Olsson, Elisabeth Özdalga & Catharina Raudvere (ed.) (İstanbul: Swedish Research Institute, 1998).

and asked if they were willing to receive me, but I never got any reply. Once I was there it was no problem whatsoever. They welcomed me very kindly, I tried to explain my errand and was directed to the right person. It was a man named Abdullah Uysal. He was very forthcoming and polite. From him I could get most of the books they had published by Gülen. Mr. Uysal also offered to try to set up a meeting with the editorial board that worked in a different office a few kilometers away. He also told me that the first publications in Swedish were being prepared, a series of brochures called *Windows towards Faith*, translated from English.

The production manager Uysal shared a small office with three other co-workers. I do not know who the others were and what positions they held, but the interplay between them struck me as very equal and I saw no sign of the hierarchy so common in other Turkish offices I have visited. Unfortunately I couldn't find any time to meet the editorial board; this had to wait until a few years later.

On Friday I went to the Fatih mosque. As far as I know, not many tourists come there, even if some odd visitors are bound to stroll in from time to time. It is after all İstanbul's first large mosque, built by Sinan the Elder in the 15th century, and is important even if it was destroyed by earthquakes and rebuilt in a new fashion in the 18th century by Mehmet Tahir.

As I was on my way in, and about to put my shoes aside, I was approached by a man who asked me in English where I came from. He told me not to put my shoes at the entrance—they could easily be stolen. He led me to a corner of the mosque where my shoes would be safe and asked me to sit down while he, who was a *profesör*, would inform me about the mosque. He didn't listen much to me and pedagogically explained what a Prayer niche (*mihrab*) was and reported other basic facts about the contents of the mosque, including how high the ceiling is.

After asking me once again where I come from, he took out some Swedish coins from his pocket and asked if I could change them for him. When it turned out I didn't have any correct change he suggested I could give him ten lira and said the difference would go to the mosque. I probably looked a bit skeptic so he fished out two rosaries that I would get from him, one for me and one for my mother.

How is it viewed to cheat tourists inside a mosque? The man claiming to be a *profesör* (teacher), whatever that might mean in this context, greeted the janitor sitting at the entrance in an amicable way. Of course I cannot know if the money went to the mosque or not, even if I strongly doubt it. But who am I to judge him? If he really cheated me God will take care of that, will He not? Especially if he plays his game inside God's house. Maybe he was so secular that he didn't care about such dimensions.

I stood there with my doubts and my two rosaries. Of course, I did take his coins and rosaries. How could he know it was my mother's 65th birthday that very day? Why would I for the very first time, as far as I can remember, receive a gift explicitly for my mother? Would that not be providence?

I took the bus back to Taksim afterwards. It was packed and I had to stand all the way. As I stood there I started to wonder about two things: People are much more physical in Turkey than in Sweden. Men can sit and put their arms around each other, talk up close with what to me looks like an almost amorous gaze. At the same time I know that anyone would dare to display homosexuality so openly, outside of the trendy clubs and cafés in İstiklal.

As said, the bus was packed. At one stop a man with a reusable ticket pressed himself in through the back doors. Reusable tickets are in the form of a small metal stud in a plastic casing. To register your ride, you hold it up at a machine that goes "blip" when you get on board. This man had his "ticket" in his key ring. He tapped the back of the person in front of him and sent the key ring forward to get registered. All the way forward and back again through a 60 seat bus he sent his set of keys. Everyone lent a hand, and after about a minute he had his keys back.

That is not possible to imagine with a public bus in Sweden. Here I see a trust in the social interaction that is impressive and unfamiliar for a Swede. This makes it even stranger that one should need to hide one's shoes at a mosque. Someone saying such a thing cannot have pure intentions. So, there are tricksters here. I wonder if it is mainly foreigners they play, or if "peasants" coming to town also risk getting cheated. Probably they do not have that much to get cheated out of. And then again, I did agree to pay that ten lira, to avoid conflict, almost out of laziness. As I came down to Eyüp, I checked the prices and saw that the kind of rosary he had given as a present to my mother did cost almost five liras...

Theology

From time to time, when I sit down in tea houses or restaurants, I read through David Ford's *Theology: A Very Short Introduction*. For a long time I have been wondering how handicapped I am by not being trained in religious studies. My questions stem from my history of ideas background—maybe I misinterpret and disrespect my materials if I do not understand theology. I have been worried about that. So I have decided to read up a bit. I also realize that most general books on theology are mainly about Christianity. Maybe I do not have to read those? On Islam I am fairly well read, and know something about Islamic theology and theological studies of Islam. Even so, Ford has some perspectives to offer.

He presents a five part division of theological positions as an alternative to the common denomination of radical, liberal or conservative theologies. There are two extremes, he says, one that gives total primacy to contemporary philosophy and one that only cares about the standard interpretations of the religious tradition. The first one he terms modernity's superiority complex. He claims that postmodernity has opened up a more positive eye on pre-modern ways of understanding life. I nod in concurrence.

In between the two extremes he sees three positions. The second one takes philosophical schools very seriously and tries to explain faith through them; he exemplifies this position with Rudolf Bultmann, who worked from existential philosophy. In Islam I think about the Iranian existentialist Ali Shariati. Such a position easily lets go of aspects of religion that are not considered interesting from contemporary premises.

The third position does not adhere to any particular school but uses all available contemporary philosophies to develop its understanding of religion. Paul Tillich is taken as an example, and I thought of Ziauddin Sardar.

The fourth position gives the Christian teachings primacy, but still takes on a serious discussion with contemporary teachings. Karl Barth is the example given, and I think this is where both Gülen and Said Nursi fit in.

I am at the Akgün Hotel. One day of the workshop on resurrection and afterlife as thought of Said Nursi has passed. In the breakfast salon I found Oliver Leaman, one of the foremost experts on Islamic philosophy, and one of my first guides to the field. I had seen that he had written on Said Nursi, but I didn't expect to see him here. He is easy to recognize by his bushy beard and long hair that curl together and form a frame for his intense eyes. There was no doubt it was him. He was very agreeable and we chatted about my appreciation of his books and about İstanbul. He tried to lead me to the conference hall, but we ended up in the kitchen and I led us back to the more public parts of the hotel and to the hall we were supposed to be in. Leaman is quite a character with his bohemian appearance, and I was almost surprised to hear that he had a wife and children. My first-hand view of normality is often embarrassingly narrow, even if I talk big.

Besides a number of insights concerning specific aspects of Said Nursi's thinking and Islam at large, the most exciting aspect of this first day for me was to see the way that many Christian theologians and priests have approached Said Nursi. Several of them have pointed out that they hadn't really read Said Nursi before being invited to attend this workshop. They had neither expertise on Said Nursi, nor on Islam. Still, they had a lot to bring as they read with confidence.

I tend to get caught up with how strange these texts are to me, how much there is that I cannot sort out and derive. The other invitees seemed to read a testimony from a man who has thoroughly examined his faith through hard personal circumstances. They seemed to share some basic experiences with him in a way I feel I don't.

The Puerto Rican Efrain Agosto gave a powerful speech about his own identity as colonized and marginalized. He interpreted Said Nursi from these similar experiences and read Nursi's letters from prisons alongside Paulus' letter to the Phillipheans, probably written from the prison of Efesos. I find this method of starting from the lived experience of the writer, to read the text as a testimony of a personal relation to God, and not being that concerned about the fact that they use models of explanation taken from different traditions fascinating and sympathetic. And it is probably not that they share something I do not; it is probably about letting go of the distanced humanist pose and engaging with texts fully, honestly and without trying to be clever or to show off one's learning. Even I could do that, if I only dared.

Agosto spoke about Said Nursi's description of five types of exile in light of the experience of being kept in an isolation cell during a prison term, and pointed to ways in which Said Nursi might be read as an anti-colonial thinker.

Arif Ali Naed, with roots in Libya, talked about the importance of the Qur'anic conception of *barzakh* in reading Said Nursi. *Barzakh,* among other things, denotes the area of brackish water where a freshwater river runs out into the salty ocean—an interstice or median one might say, a kind of ghostly domain one can access while sleeping; divine dreams come from that place. The dead are found in *barzakh*, as are the ones that will live in the future. Muhammad is there, and those who dwell there have various degrees of sensory abilities left. The Prophet can hear the people greeting him in Prayers. It is vital to understand and know that he actually hears these greetings, as a person. It is not only with the Prophet that one can establish a certain contact in *barzakh*—those that are enough spiritually advanced can establish contact with all of *barzakh*. It is in light of this one should review visits to the graves of holy men (*türbes*). For example, when Nursi says that Imam Rabbani showed him something, it is according to Naed not only in his texts, but that Nursi actually experienced contact with the Imam. What Naed had to say was fascinating and captivating, but far beyond what I am capable of imagining.

After Naed, Richard Bowering spoke. He is a scholar of Islam and Sufism who said he did not have much familiarity with Said Nursi. He modestly reported what had come to his mind during a first reading. He found the key sentence of the *Risale-i Nur* to be: "I was healed in the light of the Qur'an."

Bowering said that Nursi was no scholar, no *alim*. He did not have any deeper formal education, apart from the elementary training in religious schools (*madrasa*). His exposition of the Qur'an does not follow the traditional routes. He also has a liberal approach to logic. Everything Said Nursi says is built on personal experience.

The *Risale-i Nur* is a search for answers, rather than a text giving answers. This is why it oftentimes comes about as repetitious. It is a kind of constantly ongoing Qur'anic exegesis answering experiences and events that call for explanation. It is quite similar to the reception of the Qur'an, which was also given in relation to specific events, a piece at a time.

Bowering also said that Said Nursi's interpretations seem to come from recitations of the Qur'an rather than readings and textual exegesis. Nursi recites and repeats verses of the Qur'an, almost like a Sufi mantra (*dhikr*), and in this process an interpretation comes to him. The recitation and repetition makes the Qur'an present and the actual text is transformed from text into the Word of God and thus the Creator behind these words can thus be visible, as light. It is this contact with the Qur'an and God that inspires Said Nursi's disciples, rather than the specific content of his exegesis, Bowering thought. It is not the arguments as such that are convincing. Nursi has already experienced, seen, that of which he speaks as true. This is why he can find countless arguments showing that it is true.

One evening there was a banquet with around 300 guests, of which maybe a dozen were women. They all wore headscarves, which as such is not problematic to me, I think. Of the 18 persons in the conference panel only three were women—and that, however, I find problematic. I cannot fully decide if I find headscarves to be a free choice in respect of religion, or if it is a sign of a tradition where women cannot be regarded as subjects, and for example look at men with the sort of gaze that forces women not to display too much of their beauty. Rather, I can agree with both interpretations at once.

I would never imagine that someone could have the right to hinder anyone who wants to wear any non-demeaning symbol out of free will. Even if I find that some fashion outfits further the objectification of women, I cannot forbid anyone from wearing them. Each and every one must have the freedom to choose how to dress. Also, symbols carry different meanings and have different functions in different contexts. A symbol I find demeaning and connected to the role of object and victim might, for the one who wears it, be a source of respect and self-esteem. I cannot know that. I know a lot of women who wear their headscarves out of a conscious choice and with deep pride, as a symbol filled with emancipation and the expansion of power. What meaning a symbol has for its carrier in her tradition and context is something one cannot know without talking to her.

Still, I think it is worth remembering that the Qur'an (24:30–31) talks about the chastity of both men and women, even if male exegetes have focused one-sidedly on women's behavior and dress. Putting higher standards on the chastity of women is unequal treatment and signals a denial of female agency. As Lamya Kaddor points out, in many societies today—Turkey, Europe, USA—it is difficult to hold that the headscarf is a working defender of chastity rather than an identitarian marker.[99]

I sat there and pondered upon this between the speeches, food and the conversation. The banquet closed with a speech by the Vatican consul to İstanbul Georges Marovitch (d. 2012), who also read a part from Prophet Muhammad's own prayer, *Jawshan al-Kabir*, with great gusto.

As far as I could see, the participants were truly open to meeting and trying to learn from other ways of experiencing the divine light and considering how it can be given a stronger presence in life and society.

I spent the late evening after the banquet speaking to Mustafa Abu Sway from Palestine. He talked about what he called the religious dia-

---

[99] Lamya Kaddor, *Muslimisch—Weiblich—Deutsch! Mein Leben für einen Zeitgemäßen Islam* (Munich: C.H. Beck Verlag, 2010).

logue industry in the US. Even if it receives a lot of money there is no deep commitment to be found. Those involved in these dialogues have no understanding of things like the deterioration of Palestinian living conditions. The dialogues have no contact with the surrounding political life and if the money disappeared, no one would be interested anymore. There is no commitment to the "other." It is naïve to see these dialogue activities as a hope, he claimed, with arguments similar to those of Tariq Ramadan.

We also talked about European identity. I tried to present poststructuralist critiques of stable identities. We could meet in our critique of nationalistic beliefs in any natural essence other than that of our shared humanity. During the workshop sessions Abu Sway has shown great learning and acuity. Often he saw new ways of approaching an argument through other traditional ways of viewing a certain question. As we spoke, we both realized how tied to our own traditions we were. He had not heard of thinkers like Richard Rorty or Jacques Derrida, household names in my environs. And I had only a shallow knowledge of the thinkers he drew upon.

It became clear to me how unusual it actually is to find contemporary ties between Islam and Western philosophy. They do exist, in Iran, France and here and there in other places. I started to see a place for myself: Without being an expert in Islam, I still ought to be able to function as a sort of link between Muslim thought and contemporary Western critical theory. My academic training is deeply rooted in contemporary continental European philosophy and its different offshoots, particularly postcolonial critique. In these fields an un-reflected secularism reigns; there is a pervading lack of interest in and respect for religious perspectives.

I have spent a lot of time thinking about how to write in order to promote insights rather than dry knowledge. It easily becomes a text filled with I, me, I. Besides being stylistically unpleasant, this also produces a very individualistic perspective. "I" becomes a free floating intellect navigating around independently. For me, a good life is filled with every day prosaic cares, cooking, reading bedtime stories to my children, housekeeping, evenings on the sofa next to my wife, morning routines, and picking up kids from school. One seldom sees those sides of life in devotional or philosophical literature. I have trouble fitting it into my texts as well. How should that be done, how can we show that life is no academic or intellectual pursuit? For practical and economic reasons I normally have to leave my family behind when I go to Turkey. Families with children and conferences do not go very well together.

One of the major differences between Jesus and Muhammad, which means that I find it easier to identify with Muhammad rather than Jesus, is that Muhammad was a father and a family man. I find it easier to relate to his life in aspects that I try to deepen and become better at, efforts for which I seek strength and support in the Islamic tradition.

As I spend so much time in Turkey we often talk about the country at home. My wife Lisa has also been there many times; she has studied Middle Eastern studies, teaches Oriental dance and has her own relationship with the region and its cultures. We found each other partly because of our mutual love for Arabic and Turkish music. We have friends from Turkey. In our daily life Turkish music, Turkish TV and Turkish food have a natural place. We have visited Turkey as a family a few times, we have gone to the Sultan's palace, to mosques and markets, drunk apple tea and eaten *köfte*—like most tourists do. Our children Mika and Mona both like waking up to the call to Prayer and know the essential words to get by—ice cream, water, thank you.

We talk with the children about the strong presence of Turkish flags, something that is odd for a Swedish kid, and they ask why we have never seen a Kurdish flag in Turkey, and why there are so many soldiers in the streets. The children know that I often have gone to Turkey in the service of Amnesty International and that Amnesty tries to help people imprisoned for saying things that their states do not appreciate. In my experience it is not so difficult to let quite small children have a nuanced relationship to a country. Love and criticism do not exclude each other; the children know that first hand from the upbringing they see every day. For me, it is also important to see the difference it makes being in a context as a family. If more of my experiences had come from everyday family contexts instead of from scholarly conferences and discussions I would have other things to say. Not that the experiences would have been truer or better—they would simply have been different. This book is a solo project, but for me it is still important not to live my life, nor to represent it, as a solo project. It is vital to share the things that are important for me with my loved ones, and that of course also affects what I find important. It might sound like a politically correct cliché, but the everyday care of my children and a loving partnership with my wife is what really matters in my life. Other interests always come after this, at least according to my ideals, if not always in practice. The daily struggle is to live a life where the different spheres fit together and strengthen each other. I find inspiration for this struggle in the example of Muhammad, and through reflections on the collected wisdom of the Islamic tradition. At the same time it is often on family values that the conservative strands of the Hizmet Movement grate against my own ideals. Who should (make) love (with) whom? Who should form families? What should love before marriage look like?

Chapter 14

Akhlaq: Islamic Ethics

F ethullah Gülen's ethics could be described as Aristotelian, even if he himself does not mention Aristotle or formulate his ethics in relation to Aristotle's writings.[100] But the Islamic tradition is as inseparable from Classical Greek philosophy as Christian theology is. Gülen writes that his ethics comes from the Qur'an and *Sunna*. At the center stands the Qur'anic injunction to *"enjoin and promote what is right and good and forbid and try to prevent the evil, and bear patiently whatever may befall you"* (31:17). As Aristotle also does, Gülen stresses that ethics is not a subject one should learn, it is something to be done. One of the key points of his preaching is that we should try to be model for our fellows. Ethics is to be lived, not to be talked about. As with Aristotle, the mean is a central ethical concept. In order to point out how similar the European Christian ethics tradition is to the Islamic one it may be helpful to show how closely they both relate to Aristotelian ethics.

Aristotelian Ethics

Ethical prescriptions can never be exact or universal in the way that theoretical statements can. Human life is always complex and in flux. Aristotle rejects all ideas about a good life that are not feasible—ethics must describe a life that people can actually live. His ethics does not

---

[100] Aristotle, *Nicomachean Ethics* (translated by David Ross) (Oxford: Oxford University Press, 1980). W. K. C. Guthrie, *A History of Greek Philosophy, vol VI, Aristotle: An Encounter* (Cambridge: Cambridge University Press, 1981).

explain to us what "good" really is, it explains how we can become good people.

Aristotle calls man a *zoon politikon*, a political creature, a citizen. We are all fundamentally social, not self-sufficient individuals. This means we can only live a full life in society (which is also part of the Nakşibendi ideal). Nothing motivates people to care as much as the thought that something is theirs and that it is the only thing they have, Aristotle says. This makes the family a very important base for the state; love and care grow best inside the family. All this goes together well with Gülen's insistence that one cannot step away from society. Aristotle and Gülen also share a positive view on private ownership, while they both stress that property must never become a goal in itself. The good citizen will always use his property to actualize a good life in society.

We do not need, as many of Aristotle's contemporaries thought, to have tribe-like ties in order to strive for common goals. Different traditions have a positive role as they help us define and defend a universal declaration of happiness that can guide us in our ethical choices and our political planning. This is also in line with Gülen's promotion of cooperation and dialogue as a path towards a common development.

For Aristotle, ethics is never focused on the good of individuals; it is about creating a just and good society, since no one can be truly good if society is not good. Happiness for an individual consists of living well, in accordance with the virtues, but also in accordance with one's personal principles. The exclusively human quality of possessing a thinking soul makes it possible for us to subordinate ourselves to elaborate norms. We need practical wisdom (*phronesis*) in order to evaluate these norms and see how they should be applied in a specific situation, and we need the ability to control our desires and feelings.

Morality is only given to us as a disposition, a potential that needs to be disciplined and made into habit so that we can to do what is good in every situation. Fostering good habits, good education, just laws and sound societal norms is vital. Once again we can say that Gülen agrees and finds support for his position in the Qur'an and *Sunna*.

What is good, then? Aristotle is in every context looking for harmony. A good state is a state of harmony. The mean is the norm. A number of virtues must be applied in moderate doses. One shall always aim at the excess that is closest to the mean. Concerning courage, it is better to act foolhardy than cowardly. Yet, everyone has her own personal inclination, dependent on orientation and habit. Thus moral advice can never be generalized. We recognize this idea from the discussion on *fatawa*. Gülen describes the same principle as the straight path—*assirat al-mustaqim*, one of the most common terms for the good Islamic life, the mean between excess (*ifrat*) and deficit (*tefrit*). In Gülen's argumentation, more emphasis is put on the need for a teacher, a friend and guide, who can remind us of our direction. He also stresses, in accordance with most Sufi orders, that these practices cannot be undertaken in solitude. The walk on the straight path takes place in society. Even if Gülen has never been a part of any Nakşibendi order he shares many values with the Nakşibendi tradition. A good life includes head, heart and hand, as the philosopher Ibn Miskawayh says.

Islam is often portrayed as radical, but like classical Greek ideals it is rather a celebration of moderation and quiet everyday life. As such, it is also very similar to Swedish, and from what I can understand, Anglo-Saxon public norms. And still so many Westerners think Islam and the West are bound to clash.

One prominent Said Nursi scholar is Bilal Kuşpınar, a professor at the prestigious McGill University in Canada. He is not only one of the key researchers connected to the İstanbul Foundation for Culture and Science, but he is also an expert on Illuminationist philosophy and the 12th century Persian philosopher Suhrawardi. It is not often I get to talk to people who share an interest in Suhrawardi. To me, Bilal is not only a stimulating intellectual contact; he is also a model of kindness, humor and humility. Bilal seem to have a Nasreddin Hodja story for any situation, and he sings pious Arabic songs in honor of Prophet Muhammad with a voice that can move anyone. When discussions become too stilted or too grand, he can knock them back down to proportions with a Hodja joke.

One such recurrent commentary is "eat, my sleeve, eat." It is a shorthand reference to a Hodja story. Nasreddin Hodja, who was an Islamic scholar, had heard that there was to be a banquet at the Sultan's palace. Nasreddin, who wasn't very concerned with superficialities, went there in his everyday clothes. The guards refused to let such a wretch inside. So Nasreddin went home and put on his complete official *hodja* costume, complete with distinctive caftan and large turban. When he came back to the palace, he was not only let inside but awarded a seat next to the sultan at the table of honor. As the soup, which was the first dish, was being served, Nasreddin did not pick up his spoon like all the others. He merely held his sleeve to the plate and said, "Eat, my sleeve, eat." The people sitting next to him at the table were curious about his odd behavior and asked what he was doing. "When I first came here I wasn't accepted inside, but when my caftan came it was awarded this seat of honor. This means it is my caftan rather than me that has been shown this respect and it is thus no more than right that it gets the food that is being served."

To me, Bilal seems to be a person living the morality of this story. Even though he is a professor, a keynote speaker, and an acclaimed name, he sees that much of this attention is connected to his public role. He still comes forward as a curious boy from Konya who is as interested in speaking to the bus driver or waiter as he is in speaking with a professor. This is not all that common in a country where many people of high status treat different people differently, and hardly even notice the existence of service personnel.

Actually, I have met many people in religious circles who try to treat all people equally. If the secularists tend to be uninterested in the uneducated workers and see them only as servants, the religious might rather be a bit distancing towards women who dress and live without religious concerns. At least that is my anecdotal impression.

At a conference in Kumburgaz I met Bilal's friend, the journalist and writer Fred Reed. Partly because his contacts with the Nur Movement, Fred converted to Islam at the age of 60. He claimed not to be particularly interested in Said Nursi's texts, though. He found them somewhat difficult and far from his own circumstances. Instead, it was Said Nursi's personal example and life that inspired him. Fred has written a book called *Anatolian Junction* about Said Nursi. Fred was not very enthusiastic about Gülen, though. There was nothing in his person that he could relate to, and as an old leftist activist he was disturbed by Gülen's support of the Turkish state. He found it hard to identify with the weeping Gülen.

I have met many people who have difficulty taking this weepy and humble character seriously. Many say that his behavior cannot be for real. It is foreign, and maybe also a little bit uncomfortable. I haven't met him, but I have seen him in many videos and other conversational appearances.

We can take the Ramadan sermon from the Fatih mosque in 1991 as an example. Gülen opens by saying that he is: "...Always afraid to betray you, trick you. What will I do when I am called to answer for all the incorrect things I have said? I talk and talk to open hearts, but mine is shut, weak. This worries me constantly. But a pure seeker can find gems even in dirty mud. Please look upon my words in this way."

And he sobs and cries. Is that really sincere? It is definitely a big difference from Said Nursi's appearance, who says that Ali has predicted his writings, even if he also says the power is not his, but comes from the Qur'an.

Gülen talks about his "magpie voice," and says that he thinks that if people like himself, the smallest in society, do their outmost, they can dream about the Prophet and out of love for him they can make him an example for their conduct. "But whatever I say it is going to be wrong," he says then. This sermon is about the Prophet and his Companions. Gülen speaks with the tears always near about Muhammad's avidity for Prayer as his only worldly, human desire. Still, even if he had this desire for Prayer, it happened one time that when Muhammad had set out to hold a long Prayer with his community, he heard a baby crying. He quickly finished the Prayer in order to let the mother comfort her child. Such was Muhammad's compassion and humanity that the comforting of a crying child was more important than the Prayers of the community and of the Prophet, Gülen says and sobs anew.

I am fascinated by his empathy and immersion. I do not find it fawning or weepy. It seems to me that he is really overwhelmed by the grandness of the Prophet and the enormity of God, and by our own littleness. Sometimes I do feel uncomfortable with how Gülen's compassion is portrayed. In the biographical opening to most of the English translations of his books, it says that he has such a strong feeling for creation that he feels sorrow and compassion even when a leaf falls from a tree. To me that is just too much. I cannot take it seriously.

My friend Selçuk Akti stresses that every tradition has its conventions, and that it is not strange for a person filled with *akhlaq* (morality) to be like that. Gülen is not exceptional; the image of him crying over the falling leaves places him in a tradition of exemplary men. The falling leaves are also an established image for winter and death in Turkish Sufi poetry. As is often the case, metaphors and images are difficult to translate into other languages and perceptions of the world.

Gülen has also written about crying. There are a number of different kinds of tears. The purest are those coming from belief and knowledge about God, from fearing God. To cry over hardship only makes the devil happy, says Gülen. One should learn to resist that.

> Crying for the sake of God is the sounding out of the love cherished for Him. One who has fire in the heart will have tears in the eyes; a person with eyes as dry as deserts does not have life within. Sadness and tears are the most important characteristic of God's Prophets.[101]

---

[101] Gülen, "A Season to Weep," in *Speech and the Power of Expression: On language, Aesthetics and Belief,* (New Jersey: Tughra Books, 2010) 85.

Chapter 15

Border Thinking

E ast is East and West is West. We have heard it many times. Rudyard Kipling, the author of *The Jungle Book*, said they shall never meet, and political scientist Samuel Huntington argued in an all too influential article in 1993 that they will always clash.[102] Yet in *The Ballad of East and West* Kipling went on to state that when two persons meet face to face there are no borders, no East and no West.

Today Huntington is more widely read than Kipling, and those using only the first line of Kipling's refrain quote, not bothering about the following lesson of how borders might be overcome. Huntington is far from alone in imagining an uncrossable border between East and West. He is merely an all-too ordinary representative of Western modernity, and creating and enforcing borders is a fundamental practice of modernity. It is really this either-or logic that I am trying to get away from, since it assumes that there is an objective and uninterested border maker. This very approach transforms the world's multifarious life into objects that can be sorted and categorized. Men are transformed from unique living persons into mere examples of their category.

Making distinctions between different phenomena and disciplines leads science forward. It is important to remember that. Without modern science we wouldn't have antibiotics, electricity or uncountable other things that allow us the lives we lead today. Unfortunately, the distinctions between different areas of knowledge have also had less positive effects.

---

[102] Samuel P Huntington, "The Clash of Civilizations?" in *Foreign Affairs* 3 (1993).

Politically, the transformation from medieval times to modernity consisted among other things of the creation of fixed borders between states. These borders can even be seen as a political and epistemological invention of European modernity, politically established with the peace of Westphalia in 1648 and spread around the world with imperial colonialism. In philosophy and epistemology the most influentially border maker was René Descartes, who was active in the same period. In different areas dichotomies and separations were made between *us* and *them*—this state and that state, mind and body, civilized and barbarian, either-or...

One aspect of this was developed in the Cartesian scientific theory, where an object could only have one essence, a cause only one effect. The burning of coal, for example, caused heat and energy. That was the essential outcome. Other effects could only be interpreted as side effects, and pollution was thus not essential. But in the long term, we might see that pollution will kill everyone that the coal might warm and produce energy for. From that perspective, the energy effect can be seen as only a temporary gain from a deeply destructive process.

This very simplified example serves to show that matters are more complicated than the border building, either-or thinking modernists could see. Or maybe we should acknowledge that it took a long time before the complexities left out of the very productive scientific models were possible to discern. The (over)confident belief in science dominant in positivistic modernity is related to what Gülen has often criticized under the name of materialism. "Enlightenment movements beginning in the eighteenth century saw human beings as mind only. Following that, positivist and materialist movements saw them as material and corporeal entities only."[103]

If we take modernity to be what the staunchest modernists wanted it to be, as I have done so far, we run the risk of simplifying life lived in the modern society. Modernization did not make the world modern in the way the modernists expected. But in my use, modernity is the ideology and practice of the modernists, and the borderland is the place

---

[103] Gülen, *Essays – Perspectives – Opinions* (New Jersey: The Light, 2004), 79.

where its shortcomings and abuses become visible. Another way of stating that modernist modernity has never been hegemonic can be found in the sociological concept of multiple modernities—there have always been many different ways of being modern. From a sociological perspective, I find that concept fruitful, but from a more philosophical perspective, modernity is useful as a marker for the ideology and practice of Western expansionism.

Gülen as a Border Transgressor

But Gülen is not merely a critic of *them*, over on the other side of the civilizational borders. His critique is directed at both sides.

> ... the East's and West's civilizations have existed separated from each other. This separation, which should not have occurred, was based on the former's retiring from intellect and science, while the latter retired from spirituality, metaphysics, and eternal and invariable values. As a result, the last centuries of this millennium have witnessed disasters that are hard to believe.[104]

The border set up between East and West is a false one, Gülen implies. To say that science is Western and spirituality Eastern is just a symptom of the border creating mentality. The separation should not have occurred, he says. It was an invention. As with all inventions, it had a purpose connected to the time and place of its invention. I would argue that one important purpose of the invention was to prove the West's superiority. But its time has run out, and there is no room for it today.

> Borders are set up to define the places that are safe and unsafe, to distinguish *us* from *them*. A border is a dividing line, a narrow strip along a steep edge. A borderland is a vague and undetermined place created by the emotional residue of an unnatural boundary. It is a constant state of transition. The prohibited and forbidden are its inhabitants.[105]

---

[104] Fethullah Gülen, "At the Threshold of a New Millennium," *The Fountain*, March 2000.

[105] Anzaldúa, *Borderlands*, 25.

The words above are taken from Chicana feminist Gloria Anzaldúa. She claims the borderland as a place where one can have a full identity, not accepting all those that say that purity and belonging to only one side are essential for a qualitative identity. In her writings, the borderland becomes a place for a new understanding of traditions, heritage and identity. She is from the indigenous Mexican mestizo population of south Texas that came under US rule after the wars between the United States and Mexico in the middle of the nineteenth century. Her borderland is Anglo-Spanish-Aztecan. Her story is tied to her very special biography. But her example can be inspiring in the analysis of many other places.

Turkey is often called a bridge between East and West, a place where they meet and intermingle. Tourist guides are full of those kinds of expressions. We could, to sound more academic, instead call it a borderland. A borderland where East and West are wrapped around each other in layer upon layer such that it is impossible to say what is what: Hittite, Greek, Roman, Byzantine, Seljuk, Ottoman, Turkish, Central Asian, Kurdish, Muslim, Sunni, Alevi, Balkan, Middle Eastern, Mediterranean, European, and many other layers. If Turkey is a borderland, Fethullah Gülen can be called a person who has developed and preached a border gnosis that takes us beyond the confrontational understanding of East and West.

But Turkey is not the only borderland, perhaps just a more obvious one. At least in a metaphorical way, today we are all living in borderlands, a global border village where no one can live a life sheltered in one tradition only. If we could only escape from the comfortable self-absorption of fixed identities, and instead live in the multilayered present, we might see that bordering is a modernistic and even unnatural practice. Many on each side of the imagined East-West divide, be it a Sayyid Qutb or a Hindutva man, or a Donald Rumsfeld or a staunch Kemalist, will of course cling fervently to the fixed identities guarded by the border and its barbed wire. They want to remain "safe" and only mingle with those who are the same as they are.

Fethullah Gülen, on the other hand, has devoted much of his time and effort to mingling with *them*, and it could be said that he has seen the borderland as a place to meet *them* and dialogue with *them*. Since the borderland is an undetermined place, it is a place where something new can come into being. The bright future of the new millennium that Gülen speaks so often about is for him not a return to something pure and forlorn within the established borders, it is something new and transgressive. "Giving up their centuries-old clashes, these two worlds should come together for a happier, more peaceful world."[106] For Gülen, religion will be the foundation for a new and happier world; the revelation sets parameters for such a world. So even if Gülen is an advocate of dialogue and a spokesman for everyone's place in a global civilization of love and tolerance, he still has a firm normative ground for his message.

> Religion reconciles opposites that seem to be mutually exclusive: religion-science, this world-the next world, natural-Divine Books, the material-the spiritual, and spirit-body. Religion can erect a defense against the destruction caused by scientific materialism, put science in its proper place, and end long-standing conflicts among nations and peoples. [...] The goal of dialogue among world religions is not simply to destroy scientific materialism and the destructive materialistic worldview; rather, the very nature of religion demands this dialogue. Judaism, Christianity, and Islam, and even Hinduism and other world religions accept the same source for themselves, and, including Buddhism, pursue the same goal.[107]

As said, Gülen has special experiences that make him able to be transgressive and inclusive. His Turkish experience of modernistic, Westernistic Kemalism and a deeply rooted and familial Islamic tradition give him a two ways of seeing the world. As he says himself: "We have one side in common with Europe and one side in common with the Muslim world."[108] He uses that double belonging to argue for his cause from both sides. He is as firm in his critique of the lack of intellect and science in the Islamic tradition as of the materialistic denial of the spiritual in the Western tradition. He shows that there is a Western coun-

---

[106] Gülen, *Advocate of Dialogue*, 58.
[107] Ibid., 241–242.
[108] Gülen, *Global Civilization*, 148.

terpoint to the materialistic strand and tries to argue for a different and truer Western canon in contact with Platonist and Christian thinking. In this non-materialistic canon he places thinkers like Plato, Descartes, Pascal, Leibniz, Kant, Hegel, Bergson and Heisenberg. With this broadened Western tradition he can argue against the materialist imitators of the West, who, he says, are always more radical in their borrowed modernist attitudes. The Westerners in the East are thus trying to imitate a fake image of the West.

But what role do European thinkers play in Gülen's message? It is difficult to see that they have any part in shaping his arguments. Here and there in his writings he invokes their names to strengthen his point against those who believe that science must equal materialism and atheism. "The worldly allusions derive their specific meaning through their existence within the sacred universe of God and the Ultimate Truth that stands at its center," one could say.[109] The quote is taken from an analysis of Martin Luther King's rhetoric. To me, Gülen's and King's use of the Western non-theological canon are very similar. As Fredrik Sunnemark argues in his analysis of King's rhetoric, it is hard to find any detailed content in the references made to the authorities of the modern canon. They are not building blocks for the argument. It might seem as if King's use of literary references simply fills the function of ornamentation. But that is a too simplified understanding, Sunnemark says. The allusions are a method of legitimizing the civil rights movement's claim to righteousness. But it is not a philosophical method; it is a preacher's method. The allusions are significant and important, but they are part of a rhetorical establishment of a theological argument formed without their participation. Therefore a rather superficial understanding of these sources can make do, for both preacher and listener. The same can be said of Gülen and his style of argumentation.

Materialistic conclusions drawn from European philosophy and European scientific developments are not only contrary to the message

---

[109] Fredrik Sunnemark, *An Inescapable Network of Mutuality: Discursivity and Ideology in the Rhetoric of Martin Luther King, Jr.,* (Göteborg: Acta Universitatis Gothoburgensis, 2001).

of the Qur'an, but they are not scientifically valid or representative of the most important philosophers of European modernity such as Descartes, Leibniz, Kant and Hegel, Gülen states in a passage in *Towards a Global Civilization of Love and Tolerance*. As said, these thinkers are mobilized as religious and anti-materialistic. But it is not clear what it is in their work that has led Gülen to this conclusion. Gülen's rhetorical method can be contrasted with that of Ali Ünal, one of Gülen's key translators and heirs.

"Seeing religion and science or scientific studies as two conflicting disciplines is a product of the Western attitude toward religion and science," writes Ünal.[110] This is the same claim as we find in Gülen. But Ünal goes on to develop an argument based on Western sources. It was already with Paul that the Christian relegation of nature and this world to a lesser domain started, Ünal claims. He traces the denial of this world through Western Christian history and argues that this was what led to a rift between rationality and religion. There is also a somewhat closer discussion about Descartes' role in the development of this dualism, which leads Ünal to a different opinion than Gülen. For Gülen, it is important that Descartes was a Christian and thereby anti-materialistic; in Ünal's view, Descartes strengthens the dualism inherent in the Christian tradition that leads to materialism and Western modernity's disconnection from religion.

Border Gnoseology

Gülen can be seen as a border thinker, as a producer of border gnosis, but what does that mean? It might sound like pure jargon, theoretical gibberish.

Argentinean philologist Walter Mignolo has theorized about borders and developed the concepts of border thinking and border gnoseology. According to Mignolo, it is often necessary to change the terms in order to change the content of a discussion.[111] I see some affinities

---

[110] Ünal, Ali, *Islam Addresses Contemporary Issues*, (New Jersey: The Light, 2006) 58.
[111] Walter D. Mignolo, *Local Histories/Global Designs: Coloniality, Subaltern Knowledges, and Border Thinking* (Princeton, NJ: Princeton University Press, 1999).

between Mignolo's and Gülen's critical ambitions. Or maybe more to the point—Gülen can be seen as a representative of a break with modern/colonial epistemology that Mignolo is trying to encourage and develop.

Mignolo develops the concept of gnosis as an alternative to episteme. These terms are both Greek words for knowledge. But in the modern international academic language, gnosis has been connected with Gnosticism and the search for knowledge about God. The rational knowledge revered by modernity's big philosophers such as Descartes, Kant and Husserl is episteme, which is connected with empiricism and rationalism. But Mignolo argues that that division was made not only in the interest of philosophy and science, but also excluded a lot of local, non-Western knowledge that was articulated in different, maybe non-textual ways, and therefore were not recognized as epistemic knowledge by modernity. A lot of important local knowledge was thus lost forever, but it is still possible to reactivate some of it.

Episteme was reserved for the West and gnosis for the East. That is of course a simplification, but a simplification that in time became productive in the sense that the two sides of the dichotomy came to reproduce themselves in line with it. Gnosis was non-Western and therefore not wanted in the West. Episteme was Western and therefore not understandable or useful to the East. And so the prejudice and empty phrase that East is East and West is West was born. It implied that we should stick to our respective fields of expertise and learn to live with the fact that we cannot understand each other. For the hardliners, it meant that the others should be conquered and ruled, or even that they had no right to live.

It is very important to note that the reverence for episteme and the dislike of gnosis grew hand in hand with colonial expansion. Among the radical propagators of epistemic fundamentalism were those who Gülen criticize as scientific materialists and Bediüzzaman Said Nursi called students of philosophy and positivists. Mignolo rather calls them propagators of colonial knowledge, to emphasize that this knowledge was used to gain control over nature and other peoples, by suppressing other ways of knowing. To escape from this version of colonial modernity Mignolo wants to resurrect the concept of gnosis with a meaning covering both *episteme* and *doxa* and use it so that Western philosophy no longer will be allowed to judge other forms of knowledge. Instead, different ways of knowing can suit different times and different places, and there is no need for a totalizing system of all knowledge, where they can simply be put in boxes.

Border thinking, or border gnosis, is thinking and knowledge produced from the borders of colonial modernity, knowledge that recognizes the colonizing aspects of what has been seen as true knowledge (episteme) in mainstream modernity, and uses local resources to confront and alter that knowledge in order to know the particularities of life lived in that setting better.

The first criterion for a border thinker is that (s)he cannot be an unproblematic part of the center, nor entangled only in a local tradition. Fethullah Gülen fits very well into Mignolo's description, even if Gülen comes from a different background and position than the authors Mignolo deals with.

The concepts of border thinking and borderland should be read deconstructively. All thinking is in some way border thinking. There are no uncomplicated national identities, there are always cultures living without care for national borders. It is a myth that there are people who have ever felt themselves altogether at home in European rational modernity. To understand this we could make a broad use of the concept of intersectionality.

Intersectionality is a concept developed within feminist theory, at first by women of color as a way to show how mainstream feminists have tended to universalize the experiences and conditions of white middle class women in theories of gender oppression. To stress the fact that there are factors besides gender that make up the specific way any person is limited by her situation, feminists of color developed the concept of intersectionality.[112] Categories like gender, race and class are simultaneous and intersecting, and any one of them cannot be said to

---

[112] L Gillman, Beyond the Shadow: Re-scripting race in women's studies. *Meridians: Feminism, Race,Transnationalism* 7, no. 2 (2007).

take priority or be more fundamental. They always intersect in any particular and localized situation. Many of those who use the concept of intersectionality also stress that categories aren't fixed—the understanding of gender or race is always construed in complex relation to other factors. The different factors in play always make up each other. A broader use of the concept of intersectionality has been criticized, because it often misses that the concept was used to analyze oppression and power. It is a concept for seeing and analyzing the intersections of different power structures, not merely a metaphor for multicultural identities.

I want to use the concept to bring in power as a factor in the analysis of the borderland. Along some axes Gülen speak from above, along others from below. He is male and partakes in a patriarchal discourse from the dominant perspective. But he is Muslim, and as such speaks from the unprivileged side of Turkish official identification. Very few persons are privileged in all sections; a binary opposition between in and out is too broad, and an underdog perspective on one axis cannot be universalized as a representation of the oppressed as such. This application of the concept of intersectionality is not all together true to its feminist intentions; the gender axis is invisible in this article. With that acknowledged, I still think the concept is important to highlight the power relations in the borderlands.

Universalism and Border Thinking

Mignolo's insistence on different ways of knowing puts universalism into question. If there is no universally valid knowledge, can there be any universal values? If border thinking is opposed to universalism, then Gülen can hardly be a border thinker. His message is definitely universalistic. Also, in this analysis do we have to release ourselves from an over-dichotomous understanding of a choice between absolute universalism and absolute particularism? The opposite of universalism is situatedness, rather than particularism. There might be universal values, but every attempt to express them will be tied to the time and place where the attempt takes place, it will be colored by what Mignolo calls its loci of enunciation. German sociologist Ulrich Beck has coined the term contextualized universalism to describe a similar position.[113]

The emancipatory power of border thinking lies in the dual vision it upholds; the border thinker is more able to see the situatedness of every expression. Thinking done in the borderland might still spring from universal values, but it will be aware of the impossibility of speaking for everyone. Therefore the border thinker will need to dialogue with others to see, and show respect towards, other localized understandings of the universal values.

Border Dialogue

A dialogue must start with differences (or we will have monologue) and a belief in the possibility that we can indeed understand each other. We must break with the empty phrase that East is East and West is West. First and foremost we are all human beings. In Western epistemology there has been a dominant tradition to separate the understanding of non-Westerners to special fields such as anthropology. In anthropological philosophy, a branch of philosophy discussing the possibilities of understanding other peoples, it has been common to state that it is something different to understand a person or a custom from another tradition. For example: It might be hard for me as a Swedish historian of ideas to try to relive the thoughts of Aristotle, but to try to understand an African sage is utterly impossible since we do not share the same *we*, which Aristotle and I are assumed to do. Such a view makes true dialogue impossible and therefore meaningless. That is the stance of those protecting borders.[114]

There are of course representatives of a similar position from Eastern countries. But I am not the most fit to give examples of them. To them Gülen says: "Islam is the religion of the whole universe. That is, the entire universe obeys the laws laid down by God, so everything in the

---

[113] U. Beck, *Risk Society: Towards a New Modernity* (London: Sage, 1992).

[114] A. Motturi, *Filosofi vid mörkrets hjärta: Wittgenstein, Frazer och vildarna*, (Göteborg: Glänta Production, 2003).

universe is 'Muslim' and obeys God by submitting to His laws."[115] His message goes out to all humanity. We all come from the same place and therefore we can understand each other. The differences are only on the surface; essentially, we are all the same.

Another requisite for dialogue is that we do not think that a person or a tradition can only speak for themselves. Walter Mignolo might be called a postcolonial critic. One of the main aims of postcolonial critique is to show that the urge to gain knowledge of non-Westerners has often been used to conquer, rule and diminish them. It is easy to jump to the conclusion that any attempt to seek knowledge about another person or culture is a way of suppressing them. The next logical step is to say that no Western Orientalist or Islamologist can understand Islam, that only a Muslim has the right to talk about Islam. But the just, moral imperative that everyone should have the right to speak for themselves does not imply that everyone can *only* speak for themselves. This would lead to a position holding that we cannot represent someone else's rights and thus takes away the possibility for engagement for others and for humanitarian solidarity. Those who are too oppressed to be heard cannot gain any rights if that view is put into practice. It would lead to an egoistic and cynical world.

But Gülen is no advocate of that kind of misguided respect for the other. As we have seen, he takes the right to argue from both sides of the border, a must in a real dialogue.

But what are these "sides of the border?" What are East and West? What is a civilization? Both Gülen and Samuel Huntington speak of civilizations. If we assume they are not comrades in arms, it is important to see the differences in their understanding of what the term civilization denotes.

The word civilization (Turkish: *medeniyet*) has more than one meaning. According to English dictionaries the main meanings are 1. The state of being civilized, 2. Culture, 3. Cultural entity. In Turkish *medeniyet* covers roughly the same meaning of being civilized and as *Redhouse* puts it: "the sum of those qualities that give a society its particu-

---

[115] Gülen, *Essays—Perspectives—Opinions,* 18.

lar character." In both languages it is connected with the root "civic" or *medeni*, used in concepts like civil law, or *medeni hukuk*. *Medeniyet* is derived from the Arabic *madaniyya* and even if the meaning given in the dictionaries are rather similar, the Arabic origin unavoidably has different connotations than the concept of civilization arising from the Enlightenment, as it stands opposed to barbarism. Instead of the dominating opposition to barbarism and a connection to Roman *civitas,* we have in the Arabic concept a linkage to the Medina of the Prophet and his Companions. They lived a truly civilized life. If that etymology is taken seriously, we might read Gülen's extensive use of *ahadith* as an important part of his conception of global civilization of love and tolerance.

A major problem with the talk about civilization is that the different meanings often are intermingled and the descriptive use of civilization for different cultural entities in the world often becomes linked to an understanding of a hierarchy according to those entities' different level of civilization. The scale for that leveling is of course often the Western civilization's extremely chauvinistic image of itself as being guided only by liberty, equality, reason and democracy. Only in the West is there culture. Only in the West is there true civilization.

One of the major proponents for the importance of civilizations in understanding the present state of the world is infamous Samuel Huntington. In the context of my discussion, it is not so important whether one accepts his argument for the inevitable clash of civilizations or not. It is more important to scrutinize his definition of civilizations. In my view he would be just as mistaken even if his thesis was "the peaceful co-existence of civilizations." That is because he is committed to the East-West dichotomy, to the barbed wire border.

Every civilization has its own unique core values and cannot understand any other civilization, he says. It is the same stance as the one shown in anthropological philosophy. Even if Huntington wasn't militaristic, his definition of civilization can never lead to understanding or real dialogue. The most positive option within that conception of civilizations is some kind of exotic interest in those whom we can never understand. As we can see, this is far from Gülen's stance. His concept of civilization cannot be the same as Huntington's. But what is the content of his concept? Unfortunately it is not easy to figure out, since he uses civilization in a rather broad and undistinguished way. Gülen's concept of global civilization seems to refer to the state of being civilized, but also that the world will come together in one civilization. This is possible because we already are essentially one and living under the rules of God, our Creator, according to Gülen.

Can this ideal be called border thinking? If the borderland becomes global then there are no borders any more. But let us return to the difference between Huntington and Gülen. Huntington argues that the West is the only civilized civilization. I would interpret Gülen's global civilization as something that can only be realized in the borderland. It is realized by the coming Golden Generation[116] educated within the Hizmet Movement, and their special power comes from the fact that they are brought up in a borderland. Of course, this takes the notion of borderland from its localized setting in the southern United States and transforms it into the broader concept-metaphor of a global borderland hinted at earlier. Everyone can share the experience of living in a borderland, and in that respect everyone is part of the same global entity. But the understanding of that entity is always colored by a specific local experience. Even if this is a possible interpretation it would hardly be endorsed by either Mignolo or Anzaldúa; they would most probably find it too utopian.

One of the important aspects of Turkish Islam highlighted by Gülen is the importance of love and tolerance. That is the Sufi strand of Islam. Like mystics in all religions, the Sufis seek the experience of oneness with God and are less prone to border building and sectarianism. Since we are parts of the same whole, we belong to the same creation. Civilizations in the meaning of cultural entities are just different ways of expressing life in this creation. Every civilization has developed some knowledge and understanding, but often failed to see that it was only a partial understanding. But from the mystical perspective, they are not

---

[116] "Gülen envisions a Golden Generation that is well-educated in the sciences and well-rounded in moral training." Yildirim, Y. and S. Kirmizialtin (2004). "The golden generation: integration of Muslim identity with the world through education." The AMSS 33rd Annual Conference. Virginia USA.

dichotomous but complementary. We can sing different harmonies in the same song; describe different parts of the same elephant; if we break all the cups, the water will be one. There are countless images that express this belief that the ultimate truth is Unity. "Sufism is the way of being God's friend," Gülen says and makes Sufism a very natural part of Islamic life.[117] There is no tension between the exoteric and the esoteric aspects of Islam or religion as such in Gülen's writings.

Mignolo is a Latin American leftist and he mainly reads and uses other thinkers with a leftist approach. Gülen is a preacher more connected to the political right, and builds his message from Islamic sources. But they are both deeply committed to furthering dialogue and respect between different traditions of knowledge. The fact that they come from perspectives often seen as opposing each other, as maybe the main opponents, is interesting and might shed light on their respective views on dialogue. Are there hidden borders? Can there be dialogue between these perspectives?

I think that the mystical can be a meeting place and a starting point. From a postmodern point of view, mysticism can be seen as a rational humility towards the complexity of the world. There are things we cannot know, that others might have come closer to by other means than epistemic knowledge. From a religious point of view, mysticism opens a curiosity about how others have experienced and explained the ungraspable mystery of God.

But dialogue does not have to be only altruistic and cute. The Jewish Rabbi Reuven Firestone takes his theoretical departure from the Qur'anic verse "*So strive as in a race in good deeds*" (5:48).[118] Today religions are, whether they want it or not, functioning in capitalist societies. The culture of capitalism has made the entire world seem like a market. Individuals are consumers and even democracy nowadays is a competition between parties and ideas promoted in an open market. In pre-modern times, religions functioned as monopolies that claimed

---

[117] Gülen, *Advocate of Dialogue,* 259.
[118] Reuven Firestone's presentation was made at *Muslime Zwischen Tradition und Moderne* in Potsdam in May 2009.

spaces where they were the only actors. Today this is no longer the case, and even religions must appear attractive in dialogue and competition with other religions. And all markets have a common interest in increasing the importance of its industry, Firestone claims. The car industry works together to show the importance of cars. Therefore also religions should work together to arrive at the highest possible understanding of the importance of religiosity. To cooperate effectively, one needs to know one's fellow actors, one's competitors. Rabbi Firestone's proposition for dialogue thus does not require any belief that the other has something vital to teach, other than how to market the product effectively. Or so it seems. Then again, it is striking that he finds his theoretical ground in the Qur'an, which he quotes with an excellent Arabic pronunciation.

With border thinking, I felt I had found a way to engage my ideas in a more personal way. The efforts to express this met criticism from scientific editors who thought I departed too much from standard academic prose. It was not possible to articulate the long theoretical reasoning behind this way of writing in every article. I didn't know how to explain why I felt I had to be more personally present in my text than the social science paradigm allows.

During this period I visited Ankara on several occasions to manage the Amnesty International project we had drafted in İstanbul. I spent the days just before Christmas in 2008 in Ankara. One evening I sat in a bar with a notebook and a beer. I started outlining a skeleton for a book on contemporary Turkish Islam. I wanted to find a new expression. I was no longer employed in the university and felt I could now write the way I wanted. I tried the poetic format, as it is well suited to when one sits and lets the mind stroll freely.

Intermission: Reflections of an Islamophile (nasheed)

The very first years:
He was my age
Went to the mountains to have some peace,
but Gabriel disturbed him, unrelentingly

"You are something else.
Stand up in front of them all, and Read."
"I do not know how to read."
Read. Read, read, read, read!
Hesitation, uncertainty and fear.
Khadija became the structural wall.
Attester of the call,
co-interpretor and support (*qawwam*).
The allied,
facing scorn, ridicule and derision.
Big guy,
believes he has met an angel...
Without Khadija bint Khuwaylid—
no Islam.
This is what I believe.
Later:
A simple room in a mud-brick house.
A man sits on the floor holding a needle,
mending his tattered garment.
Later:
in the street, he halts and takes part in the children's game
attentively.
Goes to lead his *ummah* in Prayer.
Men and women together, side by side,
children tumbling around.
An open, humble and caring sincerity.
I would love to go there.
Where Muhammad is an example, a model;
in his simplicity;
in his care for household responsibilities;
in his constant need for Khadija as a loving support;
and dedicated interpreter of the call,
of Islam.
But, today's sincerity feels demanding and regulatory.
Women are pushed to the side and children are hushed.
Love has been given blinders,
humility is hidden behind self-righteousness.
I don't want to go there.
Where is Muhammad today?
Where is Khadija?

I have heard these inviting stories from living men.
But the model they show seems too allegorical,
revered but not lived.
The regulations,
that should stress that life is important and in earnest,
seem earnest in themselves.
Or:
Is it just that someone formed without the daily, persistent
direction
beyond himself,
does not know how to fill the forms with content,
cannot escape the felt demands,
in what should be a liberating rhythm and frame?
God knows?
Maybe I am a constantly wry Islamophile,
a scorned distant lover.
God knows,
but Khadija's man is my role model.

I do not know if I should try to become a poet. Too little of what I wanted to say could fit in such a format, in such a language. And it also makes my lack of command of the English language even more acutely felt. Still, this poem was an important experiment in my search for a style of writing. It also made me understand the importance of tools. I decided to write this book by hand. All my academic writing was done at computers. Handwriting gives another rhythm. Therefore I went out and bought some Moleskine notebooks, the kind that Hemingway, Picasso and Bruce Chatwin used. I know this was vain and childish. But the romance of it makes me want to write. And that is of course a good first step in producing a book.

Chapter 16

Am I an Islamist, or What?

When I was about to start writing the previous Swedish version of this book, hell broke loose in Gaza, with the disproportionately brutal Israeli attack in January 2009. As many others were, I was sad, angry and paralyzed.

I have worked as a tour guide in Israel, had an Israeli work permit. I have Israeli friends and it could just as well have been that I directed my interests towards Judaism. To an extent, I have also done that. Judaism is dear to me. But I also had and have Palestinian friends. I have many friends that are deeply involved in the Freedom flotilla to end the siege on Gaza. I cannot choose sides. I have become disappointed with both sides' inability to be open towards co-existence.

After a week of brutal attacks the witty and down-to-earth mystical Swedish poet Mohamed Omar, whose poems I have loved, came to the conclusion that he had to support Islamism in the version of Hamas, Hezbollah and the Iranian regime. It shook me. A person whom I read with strong interest ended up supporting a misogynic, authoritarian and violent ideology.

I was stuck on Omar's blog for a long night, which was filled with disappointed comments from his readers. Still, it was obvious that he hadn't totally lost it. Some of his arguments were pretty straightforward. The broad populace of Palestine, Lebanon, Iran and parts of the Arab Middle East can only be mobilized if Islam is an important part of the movement, he claimed. I think that is a sound observation that also seems to be validated by the Arab spring of 2011. He is also in many respects correct in observing that Iran (from many perspectives) is the most democratic of the countries in the Middle East, if you deduct Israel and Turkey. But this fact can never excuse or hide all the abuse that is taking place there, which is the fundament of the regime. It is both dangerous and stupid to try to cling to such formalistic aspects of democracy. Trying to claim that there are as many crimes against human rights in the USA or Israel as there is in Iran is either naïve or deceitful.

No matter how unjust the Israeli occupation and bombardment of Gaza is, Israel still has a civil society that is open to an extent that is and would be unthinkable in any Islamic republic.

Omar had his week of media attention, a short puff of smoke in the Swedish public sphere. Then it became very quiet around him. In 2010 he published a book called *The Islamist* where he tried to explain his standpoint. I was concerned that many people would think: "Yep, that is the way they are, those Muslims, pretending to be democratically orientated and humane, but in the end they do not care about human rights." Then, in 2012, Omar came back with another little book, called *Confessions of an Opium Eater*. He now said that all he had been saying and doing the last three years was a mistake (and then it is important to know that he had also been active with denial of the holocaust and other shady conspiracy theories). It is of course nice when someone confesses to mistakes. He says he couldn't handle becoming a public figure and a freelance columnist, having to have opinions about almost anything every day.

I must say I am quite cold in relation to him now. These last two books show that he is a bit too focused on himself. And as one columnist said about his wish to be taken back as the famed poet he was before his fall into extremism: "Do you really become anti-Semitic from being overworked?"

Still, Omar's dance forced me to think and for a while there in 2009 he knocked me off balance. Had I been completely fooled? But no, his turn showed a tendency that had been there all along, a total lack of interest in equality and gender issues. The good thing about his Islamist turn is that it made me realize that I have to have a constant focus on gender and power. Feminism is one of my foundational perspectives, and even if it can be problematic to always raise this perspective as a sort of test (as I have already said), from that point on I have been stronger in insisting on its importance. I have become a bit sterner. I can see that this affects my former analysis of the AK Party, as I described it earlier in this book. Now I would be more critical of the conservative aspects of their ideology, even before the latest turn from Erdoğan.

But—and this is very important—I am still totally convinced that the continuing process of learning can be in relation to Islam. It is only that I have gotten a stronger focus on Islamic feminist and liberation theology.

Omar has been part of a tradition of European converts related to the Shadiliyya order, organized around Fritjof Schuon, with Seyyed Hossein Nasr as a central figure today. There one can find great authors like the British Martin Lings who has written a widely acclaimed biography of the Prophet, and the great Sufi scholar William Chittick, who has translated Rumi and Ibn Arabi among others. Many of these writers approach Islam from a critique of modernity that is highly conservative, even aristocratic.

It is interesting to see the differences between Gülen's and Ling's books about Muhammad. Lings carefully follows the early sources, highlights the relation with God and tells the traditions in a language that in a fantastic way captures the reverence for the Prophet in the Islamic sources. His Muhammad is very traditional.[119] Gülen has a much freer approach. He is a preacher, and he uses the wide sea of Prophetic traditions to discuss what Islam can and should be today. Gülen's Prophet is a family man, a father who only rides into battle about one year of his life. It becomes obvious that the traditional focus on wars and the military aspects of Islam's formation is shortsighted. The battles were of course important for the survival and growth of the early Muslim community, but the example of the Prophet can also be found in all the years of everyday life, when he was an attentive father, husband and neighbor.[120]

---

[119] Martin Lings, *Muhammad: His Life According to the Earliest Sources* (Cambridge: Islamic Texts Society, 1991).

[120] Fethullah Gülen, *The Messenger of God Muhammad: An Analysis of the Prophet's Life* (New Jersey: The Light, 2006).

Like Lings, Chittick and Omar, I have also sought arguments for a critique of modernity within Islam. My point of departure however has been postmodern, stemming from a more radical critique of the Enlightenment's overconfidence about the reaches of reason.

There is a strange tendency among European leftist intellectuals that they do not want to see this arch-conservative side of some Islamic groups. I find it sad, and I think it can also be quite dangerous. One has to be more outspoken on equality and the critique of normativity, more persistent in finding the squinting perspectives. The Turkish context also carries potentials on this matter. But most importantly, it is time to bury the idea that my enemy's enemies are my friends. Being critical of the same power absolutely does not mean that you dream the same dreams about a possible better alternative.

Religion and State

There is an important difference between Islam and Christianity on the relationship to state power. Islam was tied to state power very early. Muhammad began as a Prophet of a religion and a founder of a state, while Christianity for some hundred years was more of a resistance movement, a movement for the destitute.

In the early Meccan period, Muhammad and the few people who had embraced his faith were exposed, and challenged the established order built on greed, pride and tyranny. To me it is much easier to feel sympathy for, and see inspiring examples in, that position. Radical Islam—radical in the Latin meaning of root (*radix*)—should in my opinion go back to these early beginnings.

There one can find an inspiring care and drive, more so than in the more triumphalist execution of power of later traditions. Gülen clearly formulates his message from the Qur'an and the early *Sunna*—the *hadith* (traditions) about what Muhammad and his early Companions said and did. He points out that in the first mosque women and men prayed together, many women unveiled, and that Islam would never have come about without the intellectual, spiritual and economic support of Muhammad's wife and Companion Khadija, and later in Medina with that of Aisha. With radical Islam I thus do not mean a militant or violent Islam, but a socially conscious and equality focused faith. To take inspiration from the early sources can often be seen as fundamentalism. The important thing is what this call for a return to the fundaments produces—and that can differ radically.

Gülen is most often politically conservative. But he is not reactionary, and he does not believe that it is possible to build the life that the early Companions lived and the state they lived in. Contemporary times have produced other demands and the inspiration we can take from the early Companions most be molded in today's forms, Gülen holds.

On January 3rd, 2009, Gülen was interviewed in the English language *Today's Zaman*, at the very beginning of the Gaza war. Naturally he wished to see an immediate end to the bombings. He emphasized that the attack weakened those who talk about finding "rational, reasonable and human solutions to the problem," those who want to find solutions not based on power and violence. Gülen also pointed to what he sees as the true Islamic path of always finding a third position that refuses violence. From a Turkish, and maybe even pan-European perspective, Gülen's position is hardly marginal. Others share it, and Gülen is an influential preacher that many people listen to.

To me this is another example of the danger of reducing the image of Islam to the Middle East, and excluding Turkey from the Middle East.

Chapter 17

Islam: The Women and the Men

As I have come to the themes where my own background tends to differ from Gülen's, it might be just as good to go directly to his view of gender and the role of women. One first impression is that Gülen, like his predecessor Said Nursi, has lived his life without marrying, and thus without sharing his adult life with women. Their service (*hizmet*) has been so strong that there has been no room for anything but God and the work for Islam. This is unusual in Islam, since this faith does not hold that celibacy is ideal and has instead always seen marriage as a natural part of life. Abstaining from sexuality has never been seen as a way to dedicate oneself to God. One should serve God in society and life, not in some cloistered monastery. It might be coincidence behind the fact that neither Said Nursi nor Gülen married. I don't know for sure.

Their single lives can be interpreted in different ways. One interpretation is of course that they have lived apart from women and thus possibly lack deeper insights into the conditions and everyday lives of women. This does not have to be the only interpretation, though.

Said Nursi has written about women; in the collected *The Letters* women are described as weak and Nursi comes across as undoubtedly patriarchal. He says women need the support and protection of men. This is written around 1930 and it would be absurd to demand that he should be very unlike his contemporaries. Still, I feel one has to be aware that it is always possible not to reproduce the patriarchal pattern. Khadija and Muhammad's pattern is so central to Islam that it is neglectful in some way not to see Khadija as the exemplary Muslim woman. She had already been married twice when she let it be made known to the 25-year old future Prophet that he could be accepted as her husband. In contrast to her third husband, she was wealthy and had employed him to run her caravans. She was in no need for someone to look after her; on the contrary it was she who cared for the light of the world, the Prophet of God.

She was the very first person he spoke to about his calling, she was the first one to pray with him as a Muslim, and she was the first one to stand by him in faith. Without her support he would never have dared to speak to others about what he had heard and experienced. This is what the Islamic sources say.

Still, what is important is if the current readers of Nursi can move on and use the potential for equality and women's power that is to be found in early Islam, when Muhammad was dependent on the strong, wealthy and experienced Khadija to dare to stand by the truth that had been revealed to him. In my opinion this happens too seldom. And I think all too many people take the dominating patriarchal interpretations too lightly.

According to Barbara Stowasser, Fatima Mernissi, Leila Ahmed, Amina Wadud and Asma Barlas, who have all written modern standard works on women in the Qur'an and early Islamic history, the misogynic positions in classical Islam were developed hundreds of years after Muhammad's time, primarily in the Abbasid era. In the Qur'an, the righteousness of women depends only on their own actions and choices. If and what man she is attached to has no importance in that matter. Several of the women of the Qur'an, like Jesus' mother Mary, Sarah, and Moses' mother are noble women of faith.

The great strength of Stowasser's book is the meticulous survey and presentation of all the verses in the Qur'an that mention women. She is a distanced reporter who is very clear about the broad room for interpretation that the formulations of the Qur'an allows for.[121]

An important question for the Abrahamic faiths is about the role of gender in the fall of man. In the Bible, it is Eve that is lead astray and

---

[121] Barbara Freyer Stowasser, *Women in the Qur'an, Traditions and Interpretation* (New York: Oxford University Press, 1996).

draw sin over human kind. In the Qur'an, Adam's wife is never mentioned by name, and it does not say how she was created. Instead it is said that man and woman come from the first created human being. The neglect to mention Adam's wife by name has been interpreted as a disinterest in women, but it is as possible to argue that women are not singled out as different. Adam is mentioned five times in the Qur'an; three of these times his wife is with him. In *Surah* (chapter) 20:120–121 it is Adam who is tempted by Iblis and is disobedient to God. In *Surah* 7 it is both Adam and his wife that are disobedient together. There is thus no gender aspect to the fall of man according to the Qur'an. If anything, Adam is more in focus; never is his wife given a larger proportion of guilt. This is important since woman's role in the fall has been a strong part of misogynic arguments in Christianity and Judaism.

The Andalusian scholar Ibn Hazm counts Pharaoh's wife Asiya, who loved Joseph, as a Prophet (not a Messenger). During his time in the 12th century, most scholars had become used to interpreting the Qur'an through so-called *israiliyyat*, or biblical sources. This narrowed the interpretational flexibility and often the interpretation came out negatively for women. An important part of contemporary Islam has been to go back to the sources to free itself from classical (mis-)interpretations from what is often called the golden period of Islam, when many of the doctrines limiting women's freedom were developed. What is often called fundamentalism, the will to return to the place of formation, thus has different meanings.

To me, the attitude towards women and gender difference is a sort of litmus test for ideologies and views. I understand that this might be a very autocratic test that leads to tensions and blockages more dependent on power relations and an endless repetition of condemnations rather than an open exchange of opinions. I do understand that. But I still cannot say that therefore I should not talk about gender equality or homosexuality. Saying that I stand up for what is best for people, and yet keeping silent about how the most exposed can be given room and opportunities cannot be called anything but false. And in the parts of Turkish Islam that I have seen I haven't met anyone talking from a strong feminine, feminist or LGBT/queer-position, or someone that have been genuinely engaged in expanding the tradition to cater to these groups as well. They are to be found within Islam, maybe most strongly in North-America and Europe. I think Turkish Muslims are too quiet on these issues. Then again, this is the same as with many Christian and Jewish groups.

Gülen can hardly be described as being driven by a dedication for gender issues. He holds that men and women are complementary, and that the heterosexual family is the smallest unit where a human can become a complete individual, even if he has never experienced this complementarity for himself. The family is man's natural place, according to Gülen. He also holds up the Anatolian tradition as a kind of corrective to harder fundamentalist currents. An important part of this tradition is the more equal position of women.

In his portrayal of Muhammad, Gülen emphasizes Khadija's importance. In his text "Women: a Source of Mercy," Gülen states that compassion is a part of the nature of women. Khadija's flowering as a human being came through her ability to be compassionate and caring. Women also love beauty. It is the good qualities of women that can build a paradisiacal home where children can grow up like heavenly creatures. In addition to this strong domestic task of being the central pillar of the home, Gülen also stresses that women can have other work. And apart from the domestic duties his description of the perfect woman (*insan al-kamila*) is similar to that of perfect human (*insan al-kamil*).

> Although women, physiologically and psychologically, have a different nature and characteristics from men, that does not denote any superiority of man over women or vice versa. We can think of woman and man as Nitrogen and Oxygen in the air; they are both vital in terms of their special roles and functions, and need one another to the same degree.[122]

Time and again the mutual complementarity and dependency is stressed in this little text that still ends with a reminder that as long as a woman stays within the limits set by her nature she can become a mirror for the beauty of the Creator.

---

[122] Fethullah Gülen, "Woman: a Source of Mercy" in *Speech and the Power of Expression*.

The mere fact that Gülen writes a text about woman in the singular is telling, as there is no equivalent text about man. Instead he often speaks about mankind in general. Yet, he is also careful to always stress that men and women have the same value, that women should also be active in society, that veiling is not among the essentials of faith, and that their worth is judged just like men's according to their honesty and deeds. But I still find that Gülen speaks from a place of patriarchal heteronormativity. Even his views of women's rights and women's worth are conservative, and it is one of the topics where I find it most difficult to respect his opinions.

One way of approaching the gender issue is to count the participation of women. You will find that the Hizmet Movement has many strong women engaged in their ranks, as teachers, leaders of dialogue centers and in other activities. I have not seen any systematic study of this though, and can only talk from my own observations. In many of the activities I have taken part in, there has been a large majority of men, often up to 90 percent. On the other hand, this is no different from how it is when I go to activities with Christian groups from Turkey. Patriarchal structures do not seem to be tied to religions, they are instead regionally anchored.

A more positive image comes forth if one ponders what gender roles Gülen and the movement inspire. The most common commentary I hear when I say that I write about Gülen from those of my friends who can be said to belong to the secular elite in Turkey, is that he is a crying man. Most of them have seen a few minutes from some video of his sermons, and Gülen cries, often and hard. To many it seems weak, ridiculous and wimpy when a man cries because he is so moved by his love of God and the Prophet. You could say that Gülen is not very masculine. He has never been married and always proudly talks about how, since he was a young boy, he has pressed his own pants and ironed his own shirts. He takes honor in making tea for his guests and also cooks, things that in Turkey are women's work. We have learned to respect the importance of domestic work, say some of his followers.

One of the most touching moments I have had in my contact with the Hizmet was when Şerafettin Pektaş, from the Brussels Dialogue Society, spoke during a round table in İstanbul about his experience as volunteer in a dormitory for students run by older Hizmet students. During his university studies, Şerafettin was in charge of a dormitory for younger boys still in high school. He talked about how he had taught these boys how to clean, scrub toilets and how to cook; all in all, to take responsibility for getting their daily domestic work done, things their mothers had done for them without them, as ordinary Turkish men, even really noticing it. Both Şerafettin and the younger boys now had to learn to take responsibility.

Şerafettin also talked about how he could not really sleep at night, how he went around the house and listened to the sleeping boys to hear that they all were safe and secure. This was the week before Şerafettin was to be married. I think his experiences from his Hizmet engagement has made him into an unusually equal Turkish husband and man. I met him a year later in Potsdam and he said he was a happy man, and he also said that since his wife had stricter hours at work and did not like domestic work that much he was the one doing most of the cooking. With several men of the Hizmet Movement I have discussed how my wife and I care for our children and homes in ways that I have done with few other Turkish men. Patriarchal structures work in many different ways, and they are quite strong in secular Turkey.

When it comes to homosexuality, it is more difficult. Most people do not want to speak about it. It is only with very few persons in the Hizmet Movement that I have talked openly about it, with persons who have shared my belief that it is an important question. It is so sensitive that the discussion has to be handled with great delicacy. One of these persons said that Gülen's extraordinary quality lies in his ability to talk to the majority, that he is not merely an intellectual. His will to influence the majority makes him very sensitive to what can be said at any particular moment. This means his message is slowly evolving and that questions that have been too sensitive to address eventually find room in Gülen's sermons and talks. The man I was talking to said that homosexuality is such a question that at the moment is too sensitive for the average Turkish Muslim.

Others I have spoken to have claimed that it is strange that so many Westerners keep going on about homosexuality, that there has never been a single homosexual within the Hizmet Movement, and thus it is not a relevant problem for them. I must say I do not find this argument convincing.

What right do I have to demand respect for the rights of homosexuals? As a human rights activist I cannot do anything else. That would mean betraying my ideals. And more importantly, it would mean betraying people I love. But the question remains as to what we have is a right to demand. The man I referred to earlier thought there was a possible position on the question of homosexuality, that he saw following from Gülen's fundamental views and his way of arguing. It would be similar to the argument on apostasy: Homosexuality is against the order of creation. It is very difficult to see that it is not a sin. But it is not an offense to society, and we can never know what God has planned for each and every individual life, what path he sets people on in order to give them challenges and tools for their belief. It is hard to think, for my anonymous friend, and he thought also for Gülen, that homosexuality is not a sin and that a homosexual will not be punished by God on the Day of Judgment. But God is always greater than our understanding and His ways are mysterious to us. We thus cannot say anything more than that we do not think that a homosexual life is to God's liking. But we must leave it to God to be the judge of that. We should tolerate and accept everyone's right to choose their way of life.

This can be seen as a mystical argument. I can respect that, even if I cannot understand why God would be displeased by loving and caring relations between men or women. We must let people believe that different ways of living lead to happiness, but we can also demand that those who live and believe differently are also respected. There is absolutely room for this respect in Gülen's interpretation of Islam, even if it seems that not that many of his followers would extend it to a homosexual lifestyle.

It might be important to note that there are both homosexual and gay-friendly Islamic intellectuals, who strongly support the right to be both Muslim and homosexual without shame. The most well-known is probably the Ugandan-born Canadian Irshad Manji. She is a feminist, an open homosexual and a devout Muslim. She is a journalist, active in debates in newspapers and TV, and an author. Her most famous book is *The Trouble with Islam Today,* which has been translated into over 30 languages. Manji is very critical of many aspects of today's Islam, but she firmly believes in the possibility of an open and tolerant Muslim faith by liberating from the oppressive interpretations.

Sometimes Manji is connected to Ayaan Hirsi Ali, the Somali-Dutch politician who made a film with Theo van Gogh and after his murder had to flee to the US. There are some similarities between Manji and Hirsi Ali: They are both successful young women who have gotten a lot of media attention as critics of Islam.[123] But the differences between them are very important. Manji wants to take part in freeing Islam from its oppressive traditions, even if her ambition to describe the current Islamic debate is grander than what she actually seems to master. This leads her to overestimate her own radicalism when she writes as if she was one of the few propagating a new time of *ijtihad*. As I have tried to show, the very understanding of the abandoning of *ijtihad* rests on Orientalist perceptions as much as on actual Islamic practice. Even so, Manji does believe in a future for Islam. Hirsi Ali, on the other hand, has come to the conclusion that the only path away from her oppressive upbringing is abandoning religion and admitting that God is just an evil invention. Hirsi Ali has written a number of very harsh, critical books wherein she judges all of Islam from her own personal experiences. She has become hotly contested and often called an Islamophobe. To some others who see Islam as a threat and an enemy she is a truth witness, one of the few who reveals how it really is to live inside Islam. I think both interpretations are wrong. I often feel uncomfortable when she is slashed as an Islamophobe. From her own personal experiences, she has a right to her opinion and to express the conclusion that Western enlightenment can free Muslims of their medieval world view. And looking at her horrible experiences of growing up in an ignorant and bigoted culture, I

---

[123] Ayaan Hirsi Ali, *The Caged Virgin: An Emancipation Proclamation for Women and Islam* (New York: Free Press, 2008).

find it cynical not to have compassion for her and see how much she has suffered because of that culture. She argues that the Left in the West has a strange tendency to always see the rest of the world as victims of Western oppression. Victims are pitiful, and pitiful persons are per definition good persons worthy of our support, Hirsi Ali says about the Left. Thus the Left has a double standard, being very critical of the West and very forgiving towards, for example, Muslim oppression. I think she is right, and that critique hits me too. I have this reflex, but I try to fight it without abandoning power analysis and the will to see first the faults of my own tradition in a world order producing fanaticism and using liberalism to justify an exploitation that makes its central principles hollow.

But she is also wrong when she says that all those who dream or talk in Islamic terms are as ignorant and bigoted as the ones she met when she grew up. Deep in my heart, I feel for Hirsi Ali's anger towards the superiority complex of cultural relativism. Not applying the same standards to all is treating some as inferior, as less capable of understanding what is right and wrong. "This is racism in its purest form," says Hirsi Ali. She is right, and in her uncompromising will to show this she has been important. To write her of as a simple Islamophobe is demeaning.

Still, it is important to see that she has tunnel vision. And I am the one saying this: a man coming to Islam from an angle, picking its most pleasant expressions. Thus I have had the advantage of meeting a wise, temperate and humane Islam before I came in close contact with a gender perception that is unpleasant even for me, even if it does not target me and lock me in the "virgin cage" that Hirsi Ali describes.

One should definitely not take the problems she describes lightly. It is naïve to claim that all the problems immigrants in Europe face are due to established structures. Hirsi Ali is right in insisting that one also have to see that one's own conduct can contribute to isolation and alienation.

Hirsi Ali makes a common mistake, though, and I think it is not a conscious one. She compares the practice of some Muslims, of which she has horrible personal experiences, to an abstract Enlightenment ideal. Many Muslim polemicists use the same format, but in reverse: They put the abstract ideal of Islam against Western practices of colonialism, pornography and class oppression.

If one looks at the situation in the Netherlands where Hirsi Ali had her political career, I believe that the Gülen-inspired initiatives that give people a path to express their Muslim identities as a contribution for the benefit of the whole of Dutch society have done more good than any total conversion to Enlightenment that Hirsi Ali propagates and has followed for herself.

She is too negligent of structural constraints, and she judges all expressions of Islam from her own limited context of experience. My experiences are of course also very limited, even more so than Hirsi Ali's, and not as personal and fundamentally determinant for my life path. My experiences of Islam also come from different territories of the Muslim lands and the Islamic traditions. I am from Sweden, I have mainly been formed by my experiences in Turkey and Indonesia, and I have had the privilege to explore a more intellectual, philosophical part of tradition. There is much in what Hirsi Ali describes that I do not recognize.

She is right when she says that Islam in all its different shapes is patriarchal, as are all traditions I know of. Do you have to break with everything patriarchal, or can one use tradition to disarm patriarchy? Most of the men of the Enlightenment also defended patriarchy, even Hirsi Ali's idol Voltaire. When she claims that those who read Western thinkers are seen as unfaithful to Muhammad she is in my experience simply wrong. And—she is dangerously close to use the argument in reverse, stating that those who read Muslim texts are unfaithful to the Enlightenment ideals and thus to civilization. It is sad, I think, that the discourse on Islam so often gets this polarized. The important feminist mission of Hirsi Ali loses in credibility from her lack of nuance and openness. Much of the Islamic critique of her is blatantly self-righteous and conflict-affirming.

Her work and books are important, and I am deeply disappointed that so very few Muslim intellectuals have come to her defense, or at least seen that she is something other than a simple Islamophobe. She has every reason and right to be critical of the religion she experienced in her home environment. Islam is the reason for her painful break with her family. Even if the description that Muslim parents are the only ones unable to accept the different life choices of their children is a naïve whitewashing of the functionality of European or US families.

Using Tradition to Create Change

Tradition can be examined in very different ways. One way is to investigate what the dominant, usual, established interpretation is in relation to a specific question. From this perspective, some Muslims must be said to be quite misogynic and homophobic. Still, most researchers say that homosexual practice in general has been more accepted in Muslim lands than in Christian ones. There are of course great variations, more than I know of.

If we are set on discussing the possibilities of getting beyond such problems, we can approach tradition from another perspective. One possible interpretation becomes relevant and interesting, even if it isn't yet shared by a large group of believers. Still, it is important to be open and honest about the probability that a differing interpretation will win support and become widely established. One should not underestimate how rapidly all traditions can actually change and shift focus.

This difference in perspectives is important, analytically, and also as a positioning in the contemporary political landscape where traditions are often seen as ossified and closed.

If Turkish politics is to become truly democratic, it needs to give Islam a more natural place in public institutions. At the moment this has not been positive for LGBTQ persons; their organization KAOS-GL has had difficulties with the religiously motivated sitting AK Party government. How the higher Islamic political presence affects the role of women is more difficult to estimate. It depends on what specific Islamic positions are activated, and whether some are prone to impose their ideals on others or not. Up till now there have been women who wanted to wear a headscarf and have been discriminated against in public and political institutions.

Can the Islamic tradition enrich my and other's understanding of life and society? How? Can an empathic and studious reading of Islamic texts, for example Gülen's, help me and others see the blind spots of our own traditions, of my understanding of my own tradition?

I think this might work in different ways. We can, for example, come across direct arguments on topics we find important and relevant. But it might also work more indirectly, as we slowly develop a differing understanding of the world that opens up new thoughts, emotions and identifications that in much more obscure ways lead to new positions on topics we have seen as self-evident and undisputed.

Our interpretation of the world has much to do with our identifications, and I think it is risky to identify ourselves to many dimensions with a privileged position. It is no coincidence, and yet not a necessity, that feminism is mainly formulated by women, or that the most poignant critique of the Western, patriarchal hegemony has come from those who have been partly excluded from it.

This reasoning is what explains my relativism: the other perspective is always vitally important. Traditions evolve through their counterpoints. These vary from place to place and time to time. In contemporary Sweden and Europe it might be a Turkish interpretation of Sunni Islam. In Turkey the counterpoint can politically be Islam, but in a broader perspective it might also be Alevi and Kurdish thinking. In the US, atheist counterpoints might be at least as important as Islamic ones. The main point is that it differs from situation to situation. If I lived in the US, I might have instead written a book defending atheistic positions, showing that there are more nuanced and respectful atheistic thinkers than Richard Dawkins.[124]

It is very difficult to understand what forms world views in a specific place at a specific time, and from this decide what components are important to focus on. Social life is an utterly complex phenomenon, the whole is larger than the sum of its parts and it is impossible to calculate how a change in ingredients will affect the future. Still, we all need to act from the understanding we have managed to reach, try to move

---

[124] Richard Dawkins, *The God Delusion* (London: Transworld, 2007).

on and at the same time be ready to change our minds when the outcome seems to be tipping in another direction. The need for alternative thinking is eternal, but *what* this other is might change very rapidly.

A somewhat soothing aspect is that the most important thing is to acquire a double consciousness, to have the ability to see and sense the world from more than one perspective. If one of these consciousnesses express a non-privileged perspective it is even better. Exactly what this other thinking will be is most often decided by coincidences and factors beyond our control, such as where we grow up and what languages we speak.

In my case, Turkey and Turkish Islam have come to be my path towards another thinking. I would also stress that we should not conflate all Western positions with a privileged tradition of knowledge. As a Swede, I am part of a privileged European tradition, but Swedes also speak and write a provincial language that has never had a powerful position in the world. If we want to get in contact with larger discussions and the development of knowledge, we need to acquire another language. This has always been the case, even if the language we need to acquire has changed over time.

One should also be more precise about heritage and belonging, and view these things intersectionally. Sometimes class might be a more important determinant than language. To my knowledge, none of my ancestors ever mastered Latin. Even if I was raised very close to the old university town of Uppsala, I never identified with the Academic Uppsala. I was always the farmer boy feeling excluded from the institutions of learning.

In these experiences there probably lies a seed for a dis-identification with a conservative reverence for the existing order. Almost all women carry different seeds. Most people have some part of themselves that skews against the established norms. For Swedes, our geographical and linguistic peripherality are two such a skewing factors. Often these qualities can be numbed by a European identification. What experiences we choose to stress and give preference to make a big difference.

Belonging to the majority, being identified as part of the establishment, being given access, probably hampers the establishment of another thinking, at least a radical and solidaritarian thinking. So far I have found it difficult to develop my Swedish peripherality into a real basis for another thinking. There may also be advantages to immersion in two of the larger and broader traditions. One must always stay focused on the skewedness and not be too attracted by belonging and acceptance, and thus become allied with the privileged of the other tradition. A non-Arab Muslim perspective might be one aspect of this. It was coincidence that brought me to Turkey, or rather—my desire to learn more about the classical Western tradition found in Troy, Miletus, Ephesus, Smyrna, the claimed birthplaces of philosophy. It was only when I came there that I came to know Muslims and became absorbed in the Islamic traditions.

Earlier I had mainly been interested in the Chinese tradition, and from Turkey I moved on to be a tour guide on the Li river, in Xian, Wuxi and at other classical sites of Chinese poetry and painting. After a while I ended up in the Turkmen and Muslim parts of China, where Swedish explorer Sven Hedin used to travel. Even if I am still fascinated by Chinese poetry and painting, I found my identification with the Turkish Muslims, but I cannot really explain why and how. Maybe because it was difficult to feel naturally at home in China; I always looked different and didn't speak the language. In Turkey I can be just a part of life, just another man on a bus.

Re-connection

One early spring evening I visit the local Pentecostal congregation where I live, where I know many of the people personally. They had invited me to speak about Islam. I am not used to this situation, to speak about Islam to people that have a strong personal faith, but no relation to Islam. The atmosphere was warm and open; coffee, cookies and songs opened the evening.

I made a short presentation, where I tried to explain that I was not primarily there to speak from a place of expertise. Instead, I wanted to talk about my identification with the Islamic tradition. This made questions that I hitherto had seen as quite unproblematic become important and difficult for some of the members of the congregation. To them, Jesus is God. This means that it is not at all as evident as I think that we all pray to the same Abrahamic God. Some think that they should pray to Jesus Christ, not directly to God.

If the way is through Jesus, the Son as a part of the holy trinity, I find it much more difficult to find a place for my own vague understanding of God, something akin to a respect for that which is grander than our intellect. It seems that an Islamic understanding of God is more compatible with the respect for the whole universe that I can feel and want to give a more prominent role in my life. Then, of course, there are many positions in between Pentecostal Protestantism and mystical Islam.

I also find a lot of similarities between the people I meet in the Pentecostal congregation and in many of the Muslim communities I visit. It seems as if the dividing line is rather between those who live for something that is beyond themselves, who let faith play a prominent role in their lives, who believe there will be some kind of judgment in some kind of afterlife, and those who live as if life is no more than what it is.

Chapter 18

Between Tradition and Modernity

It was time for a new conference, in the old Prussian town of Potsdam.[125] The name of the conference was "Muslims between Tradition and Modernity: The Gülen Movement as a Bridge between Cultures." All too often, tradition and modernity are presented as being a dichotomy, even as different cultures. What does it mean to be modern? Who has the right to decide if someone is modern?

In a discussion in Potsdam, Kerim Balcı opposed the belief of many secular Europeans that they without a doubt belong to modernity and thus have a right to speak in its name. According to Balcı, these self-assured modernists have a kind of password for entering into modernity. Do you subscribe to Darwinism? Do you accept homosexuality? These are not questions meant to be open for dialogue. These are tests with very clear correct answers that can give one entrance into modernity. This makes the questions awkward and the situation tends to become tense when they are posed. As a Muslim, one can easily become worried and defensive, Balcı said. One becomes a school boy set to give a correct answer to questions posed by an authoritarian examiner. Even if one doesn't find the questions very important, or thinks one is not informed enough to give a satisfying answer, one has to live up to a certain preset standard of modernity to be allowed to play with the others. One's own opinions about what modernity might mean and any other opinion one might have become irrelevant in face of these two test questions.

---

[125] The conference was held in 2009.

I was very touched by Kerim's words. He is a person I respect and like. I think it was the first time I really realized that much more is at stake than I had seen. It might even be an explanation for Gülen's shifting tone when addressing Darwinism, even if I am still not convinced by the arguments against evolution presented by either Balcı or Gülen. I still find it the most credible scientific explanation for the shapes of life we find around us. But where does the theory of evolution start and end?

I think polemicists like Richard Dawkins fire up the divisions and make religious people believe that evolutionary biologists and other Darwinists think they have proof that God does not exist, while atheists runs the risk of thinking that all who believe in God totally deny any scientific search for knowledge. Then again, it is not the role of Dawkins to mediate this dispute. As much as Gülen has a right to preach that a society where God is more loved would be a better society, Dawkins has a right to preach that a society where God is deemed as a mere human invention would be better.

What might seem odd is that I like reading both of them and tend to agree with them both. If the God that Dawkins fights against was abandoned in favor of Gülen's God, I think our society would benefit. But it is more complicated than that: In some respects they do talk about the same God and genuinely oppose each other. The God who creates that Dawkins mocks is important for Gülen, even if I can find guidance from his writings without having an opinion on such an active God.

What about me? What are the questions that make me freeze? When do I lose my ability to argue dispassionately and reasonably? I think one should take these questions very seriously. But I also think that it is almost impossible to answer them. One should be very careful not to think one is transparent to oneself. This is one reason why we need dialogue, to help ourselves see our own blind spots.

It is obvious that we always need some sort of preconception of things and people we have never met. For example, I am not an evolutionary biologist and my view on evolution mainly comes from secondary sources and is of course tainted by ideological interests that I am only partly aware of. I cannot claim to have seen the evidence for evolution, but from what I understand about sound scientific procedure it seems to me that those who promote the theory of evolution stand on more solid ground than those who don't. Still, I should always be open for the possibility that I might have misunderstood something.

The difference between an inescapable preconception filled with lacunas and generalizations and prejudice lies in how we handle new information on the subject concerned. Prejudice comes from not being able to change one's mind in light of new information. What happens when someone tells me that what I hold to be true is in fact not true? Often it is not a problem. I learn something new and change my mind. But part of my understanding of the world is connected to my understanding of myself and my identity.

To me, gender equality is very important and I would very much like to see gender roles become freer, so that there are fewer assumptions about our behavior dependent on belonging to a certain sex. If I think that the possibility of escaping gender roles is connected to the fact that there isn't any great biological difference between the sexes, I will most probably try to avoid information pointing in the opposite direction. I find it much easier to find flaws in the argumentation for differences between the sexes because I do not like them to exist. The information about equality and similarity I take on quite uncritically and thus strengthen my opinions. Prejudice is simply more on an emotional register than on an epistemological one. Rational arguments do not easily affect the beliefs that build our identity; more often we become emotional in response to such arguments, even more so if we feel threatened or accused in our identity.

This goes for all of us. For Gülen and many religious persons, it seems to happen in relation to Darwinism. To me it happens with gender difference, even if I seldom feel accused in relation to this topic. As has been said, it is very difficult to see our own prejudices. As a reader you might have spotted some of mine. If so, please let me know.

One evening in Potsdam I came to talk with İsmail Albayrak from the Catholic University in Melbourne, Australia. He is a theologian and an expert on the evolution of Qur'anic exegesis in the early period, and on the use of Jewish and Christian materials in the interpretation of the Qur'an. He is also a man who has followed Gülen's work from the late

1970's when Albayrak was only a little boy. Albayrak has written a book on Gülen's commentary of the Qur'an in which he shows that Gülen works within the classical Ottoman tradition in his methods and use of sources. A difference compared to other contemporary Sunni scholars is his use of Persian sources. Albayrak also stresses Gülen's ability to revise his thoughts and take a new course of thinking and action depending on new information and changing conditions. He talks about the different places where Gülen has worked and the phases of life that has formed his message as well. In Turkey it is not uncommon for Gülen to be portrayed as a hypocrite when he changes his opinion, as if it is dishonest to change one's mind. Instead, it is a sign that Gülen is a constant reader and that he follows the developments in society. Gülen keeps evolving his ideas in relation to a broad Islamic tradition and to the position he has in contemporary society. In this he differs from some of his followers as well as many in the Nur community. Some followers think everything their masters say is the truth, without really relating it to the contemporary context, or as inspiration to go further into the tradition themselves. Maybe activists are happy to have found an inspiration for working for the good of society. Maybe the need for constant interpretation is an academic thing? I would hope that it isn't a contradiction. I think it is a challenge for the movement to stay open to change and keep on following the spirit of Gülen instead of his exact, situational words.

On the last day of the Potsdam conference it was time for my presentation.

The Politics of Fethullah Gülen: Conservatism, Democracy, and a De-colonial Option

As was said in the opening of this book, Fethullah Gülen has been voted the world's leading intellectual, in *Foreign Policy/Prospect* 2008. His Islamic message inspires millions of followers in Turkey and globally. Some see him as an Islamist cult leader, others as a 21th century equivalent to Gandhi. My Potsdam presentation analyzed the political content and implications of Gülen's writings.

Gülen has many times asserted that he has no political ambitions. He has never aspired to lead a movement or to gain political power of any sort, he says. In that respect he is a non-political thinker, and is focused on making humanity love God. But he also thinks that if humanity starts to know God correctly and love Him, this will lead to a new and better civilization based on love and tolerance. This can definitely be seen as a political statement. The Gülen Movement is participating in education, media, social solidarity, aid, and integration work in Turkey and abroad, activities that are connected to political spheres and themes. Gülen and the movement has also been an important source of dignity for Muslims participating in modern societies, as moderns and Muslims. I argue that this is an important political impact, something that has always been at the heart of political struggles.

What is Politics?

The words "politics" and "political" can have many meanings. They are tied to what can be described as an essentially contested concept, with no objective definition. Trying to define this concept is engaging in political debate. According to Aristotle, politics is a society's communal efforts to find a good life and to solve the conflicts between the common good and special interests.[126] "The personal is political" was one of the main slogans of second wave feminism.[127] One of the outcomes of the feminist political struggle was a different and broader understanding of what can be analyzed as political that has been adopted mainly by thinkers on the Left. From this understanding follows that the secular wish to enforce a separation between religion and politics is as futile as the wish to separate private and public.

In Gülen's statements about having no political aspirations "political" seems to mean party politics and representation in the parliamentary power structure. He has never aspired to this. But then he has him-

---

[126] Aristoteles, *Politics* (Leob Classical Library, 1932) § 1252a.
[127] Carol Hanisch, "The Personal Is Political" in *Notes from the Second Year: Women's Liberation: Major Writings of the Radical Feminists (Magazine)* (ed.) Shulamith Firestone & Anne Koedt (New York: The New York Radical Women, 1970).

self said that such a narrow understanding of politics is mistaken: "Those who understand politics as political parties, propaganda, elections, and the struggle for power are mistaken. Politics is the art of management, based on a broad perspective of today, tomorrow, and the day after, that seeks the people's satisfaction and God's approval."[128]

From this definition of politics I find it difficult to say that Gülen has no political aspirations. Maybe it is that we need to distinguish between aspirations and ideas. It is true that Gülen does not seem to be aspiring to manage a movement. But he certainly presents ideas about how a good management should be executed.

So political can mean different things in different contexts, and defining the term is part of the political debate itself, as with other essentially contested concepts such as liberty or democracy.

I tried to show that Gülen does have a consistent and clear political theory that can be defined very well within the parameters of the classical Western political ideologies. Gülen has a conservative political message. His understanding that his own work should not be defined as political also reflects this conservative and more classically institutional understanding of what is political. But it should also be acknowledged that an important part of Gülen's writings is more apolitical. In *Emerald Hills of the Heart*, for example, there is a clear focus on theology and the individual. But even so, it could be argued that the focus on patience and content with the given circumstances are more in tune with conservative ideals defending the status quo than with more reformist political ideologies.

The conclusion will be that Gülen can be read as more political than he claims, that the movement may very well be described as Turkey's third power, as is done in *Jane's Islamic Affairs Analyst*, and that Gülen can be read as a thinker who destabilizes the global Western political hegemony. Gülen's political ideas are firmly grounded in Islam. The commentators who take this fact as proof that Gülen is a political Islamist, and therefore against democracy and a secular state, are jumping to conclusions that are unfounded. But, the defenders who restate the

---

[128] Gülen, *Advocate of Dialogue*, 149.

claim that Gülen and the movement do not have political ambitions and impacts are also drawing conclusions that are biased, or built on a too narrow understanding of the field of politics.

So, I will try to give a presentation of the classical political theory to be found in Gülen's English publications.

Gülen under Attack and Scrutiny: Is He Undemocratic?

In early 2009 Gülen and his movement came under heavy critique from forums such as *Middle East Quarterly* and *Jane's Islamic Affairs Analyst*, even if these are not part of the more objective main stream. It is not surprising that the hugely successful growth and impact of the movement have led to wider and more critical attention. A man voted to be the world's leading intellectual should be scrutinized thoroughly. Gülen and the movement have come to a whole new position of power. It should therefore be acknowledged that things stated in the margins may take on different meanings when stated from a more powerful position. He might have political influence whether he aspires for it or not.

In April 2008, Michael Rubin, editor of *Middle East Quarterly*, compared Gülen to Ayatollah Ruhollah Khomeini, implying that if Gülen returned to Turkey it could be the start of an Islamic revolution similar to the Iranian one in 1979. He says the "cult leader" and his movement seek to Islamize Turkey.[129] But his analysis rests on an assumption that Islamization has a fixed and unequivocal meaning. The Swedish imam and politician Adly Abu Hajar sometimes says that "Sweden is the best Islamic state now." He says the Swedish system upholds Islamic ideals such as democracy, tolerance, gender equality and social welfare. So who is the most fitting Islamic inspiration, Abu Hajar's party colleague, the Swedish Prime Minister Reinfeldt, or Ruhollah Khomeini? The point is that this is not an analytical question, but an ideological one. And Rubin does not really give us any argument for why his comparison is the most valid one.

---

[129] Michael Rubin, "Turkey's Turning Point: Could There Be an Islamic Revolution in Turkey?", *National Review Online*, April 14, 2008, www.meforum.org/1882/turkeys-turning-point

In the 2009 winter edition of the *Middle East Quarterly* Rachel Sharon-Krespin wrote about "Fethullah Gülen's Grand Ambitions." To briefly capture her way of arguing and her stance on Gülen, a telling quote can suffice:

> He presents himself and his movement as the modern-day version of tolerant, liberal Anatolian Sufism and has used the literature of great Sufi thinkers such as Jalal al-Din Rumi and Yunus Emre, pretending to share their moderate teachings.[130]

To build an analysis on the assumption that a writer only pretends to mean what he writes is an awkward method—and very hard to argue with. But as Greg Barton reflected in *Today's Zaman* in response to Sharon-Krespin, the kind of pretense that Sharon-Krespin insinuates throughout her piece would require a conspiracy involving millions of followers. It is frankly academically sounder to choose the simpler explanation that people aren't pretending, and that Gülen actually means what he has been saying for many years.[131]

Rubin might have a better point, showing that Khomeini expressed support for democracy before his return to Iran, and that Western journalists portrayed him as a positive alternative to the Shah. He thinks these facts have similarities with the image of Gülen. This might be correct, but a big difference is that Khomeini had been writing about his political visions since the 1940s, and at least with the book *Islamic Government* (*Hokumat-e Islami*) of 1970 had articulated his theocratic ideal, that the state should be ruled by a *faqih* who "surpasses all others in knowledge" of Islamic law and justice. Khomeini built his political ideals on the example of Prophet Muhammad's and Ali's reign, but the model is also very much inspired by the Platonic idea of a Philosopher-King.[132] So it is easy to see that Khomeini was not sincere in his

---

[130] Rachel Sharon-Krespin, "Fethullah Gülen's Grand Amibitons: Turkey's Islamist Danger," *Middle East Quarterly*, Winter 2009, www.meforum.org/2045/fethullah-gulens-grand-ambition.

[131] Greg Barton, "A Response to Rachel Sharon-Krespin's 'Fethullah Gülen's Grand Amibitons: Turkey's Islamist Danger,'" *Today's Zaman*, February 11, 2009.

[132] Ayatollah Ruhollah Khomeini, *Islamic Government* (New York: Manor Books, 1979) 59.

talk about democracy, and that the journalists portraying him as a potential democratic force were misinformed. Gülen's support for democracy is coherent and even after a thorough study of his writings one has to use Sharon-Krespin's insinuative method to question his sincerity.

In reply to the *Jane's Islamic Affairs Analyst*'s report "Gülen Movement: Turkey's Third Power," İhsan Yılmaz claimed in the Gülen affiliated daily *Zaman* that "Gülen has repeatedly stated that the ideologization of Islam and its use as an instrument in politics harms Islam first; furthermore, he condemns the politicization of religion. The movement has reportedly stayed away from politics." But, he later says that "Gülen and his movement have been supporting democracy, a liberal market economy, a secular state, freedoms, human rights and so on since the emergence of the movement."[133] To me that is not staying away from politics. It is a clear political stance, but it has not been advocated through the classical political institutions of the representative parliamentary democratic system. I also think that Yılmaz is closing the debate a bit prematurely. Gülen says the use of Islam as an instrument in politics harms Islam. But does that really contradict the analysis that Gülen and the movement want to Islamize society? I still think it is clear that Gülen wants to Islamize society. But that does not really mean anything specific. If Islam is the container of all desired values of democracy it will be synonymous to Islamize and to democratize society. When describing his ideal society Gülen says that:

> The Qur'an addresses the whole community and assigns it almost all the duties entrusted to modern democratic systems. [...] Islam recommends a government based on a social contract. People elect the administrators and establish a council to debate common issues. Also, the society as a whole participates in auditing the administration. Especially during the rule of the first four caliphs (632–661), the fundamental principles of government mentioned above—including free elections—were fully observed.[134]

---

[133] İhsan Yılmaz, "Jane's Gülen Movement Analysis: An Orientalist Misreading (2)," *Today's Zaman*, February 9, 2009.

[134] Gülen, *Essays*, 17.

So, we can see that for Gülen there is no contradiction between Islam and democracy, but he also stresses that Islam cannot be compared to democracy. Democracy is merely a political system, Islam is a religion, and as such contains so much more and is concerned with a whole range of fields that are not connected to democracy. But the social and worldly ideals of Islam can be compared with, and found to support, democracy, even though Gülen also stresses that

> Islam does not propose a certain unchangeable form of government or attempt to shape it. Instead, Islam establishes fundamental principles that orient a government's general character, leaving it to the people to choose the type and form of government according to time and circumstances.[135]

So Rubin's and Sharon-Krespin's concerns that Gülen is set on re-establishing the sultanate do not have any empirical support in his writings. On the contrary, he is explicitly critical of the theocratic state of Iran and of the historic sultanate as a break from the egalitarian system of the first four caliphs. Two things might be said though. Gülen does not explicitly state how often free elections should be held, so the critic's fear of a possible free election of an Islamist despot in Turkey cannot be totally countered. One can question whether such a solution is in line with Gülen's ideas, though, and quote passages like the conclusion to his analysis of the increasing global connections in today's society: "...making it inevitable that democratic governments which respect personal rights will replace oppressive regimes."[136]

The historical accuracy of the description of the rule of the first caliphs as fundamentally democratic can be questioned. But in this context it might be more relevant to look at the ideological use Gülen makes of the example.

Yılmaz is definitely right in questioning the use of the word Islamist for anyone who argues that Islam has ideals that would improve society, but he makes it too easy for himself when he leaves the question after showing that Islam should not be a tool for politics.

---

[135] Essays, 14.
[136] Gülen. *Toward a Global Civilization*, (New Jersey: The Light, 2006) 230.

The Gülen Movement as a Social and Political Movement

I think it is accurate to claim that the Gülen Movement is a social movement, and that Gülen is a social movement intellectual. I will therefore make use of a brief social movement analysis of his writings, as one method for reading political texts.

Fethullah Gülen inspires people, who then act as a movement with political implications, but not by classical political means. Creating parties is not the only way of being political. More and more social engagement is channeled through less strictly delineated social movements and networks. The debate about new social movements started in the 1980s, when "social movement" became a label for a wide variety of collective action. This debate was closely connected to the debate about the new post-society.[137] "New social movement" became a label for those movements that had been born after WWII, when political arguments were expressed in association with popular culture and identities connected to music and fashion. The Gülen Movement is not connected to popular culture in this way, and Gülen himself has been critical of the tendencies to produce religious uniforms and other markers of separate identities.

A social movement includes at least some kind of collective identity, an understanding of a collective agent, and a shared understanding that the actions of the movement have a vaguely defined goal for a different and better social life. This is a form of political mobilization.

A social movement entails a collective identity. The identity-forming processes that establish this collective identity can be reconstructed from a set of different practices. To form a social movement and a collective identity around it one must, according to sociologist Håkan Thörn, define:

a) The problematic conditions in society

b) The causes for these problems

---

[137] Alain Touraine, *The Voice and the Eye: An Analysis of Social Movements* (Cambridge: Cambridge University Press, 1981).

c) The opponents of the movement

d) Who belong to the "we" of the movement

e) Some strategies for action to solve the problem

f) A utopia, a goal for the movement

This has almost always been done in text, and these texts can be called movement texts.[138] Gülen is a movement intellectual, a writer of movement texts. Some of his texts can be interpreted through the scheme presented above. But even in the texts that can best be read in relation to this model Gülen's work is less socio-politically directed than most other texts normally seen as movement texts of, for example, the labor movement, the women's movement, the environmental movement, or the political texts of radical Islamic intellectuals such as Sayyid Qutb or Mawlana Mawdudi.

A very brief analysis of Gülen's book *Towards a Global Civilization of Love and Tolerance* using this framework can give us this:

The problematic conditions in society (a) according to Gülen are less political than moral. Despite technological gains that have led to material ease, society today is foremost a society of division that has made a break with traditional values. It is an egotistic and intolerant society, Gülen says. The causes for these problems (b) are the turn away from religion and love and the break between science and spirituality. The opponents (c) are the materialistic and antireligious modernists, and also those Muslims who deem all scientific interests as Western and therefore evil. Gülen describes a "we" (d) of loving, tolerant and educated Muslims in tune both with tradition and scientific knowledge and technology. But this description is rather broad and vague. The clearest portrait is given of the Golden Generation, which is more of a future "we," since Gülen does not count himself as belonging to this group. The strategy (e) is to educate the future generation, to make them into ideal humans. This is not direct political strategy, but it does have a political goal: the creation of a different and better society. There is also a utopia

---

[138] Håkan Thörn, *Modernitet, sociologi och sociala rörelser*, (Göteborg: Kompendiet, 1997).

(f) in Gülen's thinking: the future ideal society, the coming civilization of love and tolerance.

According to this perspective, the Gülen Movement can be seen as a social movement, and as such it has a kind of political organization. And Gülen's texts, around which it is formed, also have political significance as movement texts.

Classical Conservatism:
An Extremely Brief Introduction

Conservatism is an ideology characterized by its respect for established traditions and its wish to uphold the traditional institutions of society.[139] Often conservatism includes a critique of rationally motivated changes in society; it holds that social reform must respect the collected wisdom in the established order, and thinks that lasting social institutions can only be built on religious bonds. The state is often seen as a natural organization with an individual identity. It is a defense for the old order, often articulated in times of revolutionary political changes in society. It first arose as a response to the French Revolution, with a classical articulation in Britain in Edmund Burke's *Reflections on the Revolution in France* from 1790; in France itself, Joseph de Maistre saw the revolution as going against the divinely sanctioned order represented by the kingdom. In Germany Johan Gottfried von Herder elaborated the idea of a natural *Volksgemeinschaft* with its own particular language, law, literature and religious tradition. The nation is built in a long historical evolution that has given it peculiar form and content. Our true belonging is to our people, and a patriotic spirit is essential in human life.

Conservatism today is democratic, even though it has never been a driving force in democratization.

---

[139] Robert Nisbet, *Conservatism: Dream or Reality* (Minneapolis: University of Minnesota Press, 1986), and Ted Honderich, *Conservatism* (Boulder: Westview Press, 1990).

Mapping the Western Political Ideology in Gülen's Writings

The political conservatism of Fethullah Gülen is clear and consistent. It is also clearly democratic. He explicitly dismisses all the traditional Western political ideologies except for conservatism.

> We do not believe that anything new will emerge from the tatters of capitalism, or the fantasy of communism, or the debris of socialism, or the hybrids of social democracy, or old-fashioned liberalism. The truth of the matter is if there is a world open to a new world order, it is our world.[140]

This quote not only shows that the classical ideologies except for conservatism are openly rejected, it also articulates Gülen's project of bringing about a new world in a clearly political context. It is not only that the coming alternative will be different from the politically shaped ones, it is that these specific political ideologies have proven unable to build a good world. And I think it is significant that conservatism is not mentioned in this context.

Gülen has repeatedly stated that Islam is not an ideology, it is a religion, and it cannot be made into a political tool. I take this as an argument that Gülen can have an attachment to a Western political ideology, since Islam cannot function as such. As I will try to show, the ideological connotations of Gülen's social vision is classically conservative. In an interview with Nevval Sevindi, Gülen said that "Islam can seem attractive to both rightist politicians with its conservative ideas and to leftist politicians with its ideas on sharing."[141] But in Gülen's writings these leftist possibilities are not explored, in contrast to the conservative ones; on the contrary, he repeatedly criticizes socialism.

In contrast to non-conservative Western political thinkers who often view society as built on antagonism and any commonality as built on interests, Gülen views society as an organic harmonious whole. "When

---

[140] M. Fethullah Gülen, *The Statue of Our Souls: Revival in Islamic Thought and Activism* (New Jersey: The Light, 2005) 24.
[141] Nevval Sevindi, *Contemporary Islamic Conversations: M. Fethullah Gülen on Turkey, Islam, and the West* (Albany: SUNY Press, 2008) 64.

one tries to redirect toward a spiritual life there will always be consensus, agreement, and solidarity, whereas, if one is to rely merely on change, then one is likely to witness disputes, divisions, and even fights."[142]

Gülen sees national belonging as an innate identity and describes family and nation as man's natural communities. Women and men are viewed as complementary and therefore the family becomes the smallest unit where we can become complete. His view of societal cooperation is thus classically conservative. Different groups in society might also seem complementary in Gülen's understanding.

> All relationships authority-subject, employer-employee, landlord-tenant, landowner-peasant, artist-admirer, attorney-client, teacher-student will become different aspects of the unity of the whole.[143]

Gülen is an idealist; to create a better civilization the task is primarily about moral change, not institutional change. When society becomes saturated with moral individuals, then it will become a society of love and tolerance. There is a harmonic, organic sense of community among humans. "The strongest relationship among individuals in the family, society and nation is that of love," he says.[144] This conservatism puts Gülen more in line with thinkers like Hegel than with pessimistic conservatives such as Hobbes. But in contrast to the classical conservatives, Gülen is a modern democrat who makes clear that no one must be sacrificed for the good of the broader collective. Probably the most used Qur'anic quote in Gülen's publications is "To kill one man is to kill all mankind."[145]

Since true reform in Gülen's understanding comes from the bottom up, there is no big need to discuss the practical institutionalization of justice, love and respect.

Gülen has always been a strong defender of the state as the most legitimate form of the nation; Hakan Yavuz even calls him a statist.[146]

---

[142] Gülen, *Toward a Global Civilization*, 101.
[143] Gülen, *The Statue of our Souls*, (New Jersey: Tughra Books, 2009), 102.
[144] Gülen, *Essays*, 123.
[145] Gülen, *Essays*, 137.
[146] Hakan Yavuz quoted in Sevindi, *Contemporary Islamic Conversations*, 128.

In his constant critique of terrorism one important argument is that according to Islamic law only states have the authority to declare war. He has also been supportive of the military's defense of the Turkish state against alleged anarchist tendencies. He often emphasize the importance of patriotism and pride in the Turkish nation, something that is most obvious in the interviews with Nevval Sevindi published in English as *Contemporary Islamic Conversations*. The Turkish tradition honored by Gülen is not only Islamic; it is also pre-Islamic strands "which regard[s] water and trees as sacred and which prohibits their destruction." He also celebrates "the equal place of women in the Turkish tradition" and states that "Turks are a modern society."[147]

I can't see that he says that the members of the Golden Generation should refrain from seeking political power. But the true transformation of society can never come about if the people do not become moral. This is a classical conservative skepticism towards the possibilities of radical imposed change. Reforms must come gradually and slowly without altering the traditional structures of society. Gülen's positive view of the Ottoman state can also be seen as classically conservative. The structures of the laicist Turkish republic do not have the organic ties to the Turkish people that the Ottoman institutions had. The Kemalist project is a radical attempt to impose new and unnatural institutions on the nation. And any lasting institution must be built on religious foundations, as Edmund Burke stated in the *Reflections on the Revolution in France*. Gülen says: "As with all other nations, our essential characteristics are religion and language, history and motherland."[148]

His ideal society is the Muslim society of the first four caliphs, and in Gülen's presentation of this historical period they are leaders chosen in free elections. After their time, the leadership of the Muslim state became tied to dynasties and thus left the original democratic spirit of Islam. Islam has no despotic aspect according to Gülen; neither is there any open discrimination on who can be elected leader—he states the example of Aisha leading an army, which also opens the possibility

---

[147] Sevindi, *Contemporary Islamic Conversations*, 72.
[148] Gülen, *Essays*, 85.

of women as leaders, even if gender issues can't be said to be one of Gülen's major interests. Also in his stance on gender he is classically conservative.

Some Conclusions on Gülen's Politics, and Remarks on Intercultural Dialogues

Gülen is apolitical in that his mission is about creating good, God-loving individuals; a new Golden Generation. But he is political in that the members of this generation shall become examples for others and thus transform the world. He also has a coherent and openly stated conservative ideology, even if it represents a small part of his overall intellectual work.

Those who try to argue that Gülen is not a defender of democracy do not find any support in his writings. He defends the right of the individual and says that open elections are the only legitimate way to political power.

Gülen is a conservative democrat. I think this opens an interesting discussion about Ayaan Hirsi Ali's critique of leftist liberal Europeans' support for Islamic movements in the Netherlands and Europe. Gülen does not support the kind of repressive Islam that Hirsi Ali criticizes (and wrongfully attribute to anyone calling themselves Muslim). Gülen and his followers seem to be ideologically more in tune with the Christian democrats that the multiculturalists and leftists love to heckle. If the leftist multicultural support for an Islamic presence in Europe is seen as a Voltairian support for the right to express views that they themselves might even hate, then it is nothing awkward about it. But Hirsi Ali has a point in that the conservatism of Gülen might be more troubling to those circles, if it was more clearly understood.

Taking Politics in another Direction: The De-colonial Option

It is often said that the old left-right axis, and the classical ideologies connected to it, has become obsolete. If that is true, we should maybe analyze along other lines than trying to pin Gülen to an established Western political position, even if that was possible to do.

Going back to a statement I have already quoted a part of I will try to take the argument in a different direction.

Turks are a modern society, even according to Western references. Moreover, there is no need for Western terms and theories to be the only point of reference. There is no such thing as modernizing only in the Western way.[149]

This is another kind of political statement, and an important one. To tie politics only to the established ideologies of the Western tradition is to keep on as if there were no alternative to Western modernity. Walter Mignolo says that modernity is only the rhetorical side of the Western tradition; the practical side he calls coloniality. Today we witness efforts to get away from the modern/colonial distribution of power and wealth in many parts of the world. These are in many ways material struggles, searches for more decent living standards. But ultimately it comes down to a question of dignity. Up till very recently, it had been impossible to articulate a political struggle from outside the realm of modernity/coloniality. Today, more and more thinkers from hitherto oppressed, indigenous traditions are claiming their right to think from their own perspectives. According to Mignolo the practice of emancipation and de-colonization starts with the recognition that also knowledge has been colonized under modernity. The political alternative needs to be articulated at an epistemic level, as a de-linking from Western hegemonic epistemology. A key point in such a political struggle is free education.

Throughout his work Gülen shows that there are other ways of being modern than the Western one, he even says that "My main objective has always been to create global education, which will become an alternative to the Western model of cultural imperialism."[150] These are words that are very hard to reconcile with a Western conservative stance, even if there can be a conservative critique of capitalism and modern society as a whole. But Gülen's works are also concerned with a differ-

---

[149] Sevindi, *Contemporary Islamic Conversations*, 73.
[150] Ibid., 74.

ent scale of politics. Maybe we can say that the fact that he is a conservative coming from an Islamic position makes Gülen's political message radical in relation to capitalism and the global Western hegemony. Maybe this is also something that the European Left sees and can acknowledge in its support for Islamic movements such as the Gülen Movement.

Political struggle can only succeed when the sought alternative has a firm grounding in an ontology and epistemology of its own. De-colonial emancipation is reached in an intercultural dialogue with modernity based on a sense of dignity coming from its own tradition.

I argue that Gülen is a thinker developing such an epistemic alternative, and that the movement is a source for such a dignity. To me, that is a significant political act, connected with the most interesting and pressing global political debates being articulated most acutely in the revolutionary movements of Tunisia, Egypt, Bahrain, and Libya, but also in countries like Singapore, Malaysia, Bolivia and Ecuador. It will be very interesting to see what strands of Gülen's ethos will be taken on by the movement, and how that will develop in the coming years.

Concluding Reflections

I would like to return to Judith Butler, and her remark that it would be a mistake to think that the disappearance of religion would be the solution to our problems. In a comment on the Danish caricatures of Muhammad, she is bewildered and dismayed over the fact that so many have been so uninterested in understanding why other people have felt hurt and upset. Many secularists are so closed in their own norms that they don't even try to understand how other people think. Any deviance from their pattern of thought is interpreted in ways that strengthen their belief that others are irrational, violent and un-modern, without even taking the time to listen to the arguments. They draw all kinds of conclusions about the width and applicability of their own norms. Butler challenges the belief that there exists one single correct norm. The solution is not in finding the correct and true norm; it is in learning to form alliances to challenge established norms that narrow our freedom to choose our own lives.[151]

To claim that I in any way could talk in the name of Islam without following the foundations of belief would be very difficult. It is a great responsibility to take on a name. I was moved when reading a book by Swedish businessman Rolf Enander about his walk from Linköping, Sweden to Santiago de Compostela, Spain.[152] He was mainly out to walk and get to know himself. He called himself a pilgrim, since he had chosen a classical pilgrimage track for his walk. As he came down into Catholic Europe he realized that being a pilgrim carried a great responsibility: "Pray for me when you come to Santiago," people said to him. He realized it was not only about his own travel; others had faith in him, in his mission, and trusted in the name he had taken on.

My identification is with the Islamic tradition more than with religiosity, if such a division is possible. I still do not know if I believe in God. I now ask what people mean by the name "God" when they ask me. And I have come to understand that most of what is important in life can be covered by this name. I have more and more faith in religious people. I admire many of them for their honesty and their sincere struggle to lead a good life. I think European society has a lot to learn from these Muslims and Christians, I know that at least I have a lot to learn. Those interested in leading a moral life have a lot to learn from engaging with the religious traditions, for example with Islam. And I do believe in a sensible humbleness for everything that evades our understanding and control, in reverence for life, and in respect for our modest abilities to predict and construct our own futures. Still, we have an inescapable responsibility to try as hard as we can to build a just and loving world. Islam has helped me understand this.

Thank you!

---

[151] Judith Butler, "The Sensibility of Critique: Response to Asad and Mahmood" in *Is Critique Secular? Blasphemy, Injury and Free Speech*, ed. Talal Asad (Berkeley, CA: University of California Press, 2009).

[152] Rolf Enander, *Vägen till Santiago de Compostela* (Stockholm: Hjalmarson & Högberg, 2005).

I would never have been able to write this book without all the kind and generous people who have shared their experience, time and knowledge with me. Most of all this goes for my wife Lisa Grinell, and our children, Mika and Mona. They make me complete. More specifically for this work: Abraham Garis, Ayşe Kızıldağ, Barbara Stowasser, Batool al-Tooma, Beatrice Hansson-Karakoca, Bilal Kuşpınar, Bill Park, Cemal Uşşak, Claes Ekenstam, Dirk Ficca, Eda Hatice Farsakoğlu, Elba Mammadli, Emel Öz Firker, Emel Üresin, Ercan Karakoyun, Eva Ingemarsson, Eva Mattson, Faris Kaya, Fatma Dişli Zibak, Fred Dallmayr, Fred Reed, Greg Barton, Gunnar Mattson, Gülden Gürsoy, Gürkan Çelik, Göran Larsson, Hakan Berberoğlu, Hakan Yeşilova, Hans Leander, İhsan Yılmaz, İlknur Kahraman, Ingvar Oljelund, İsmail Albayrak, Jan Bärmark, Jonathan Lacey, Kerim Balcı, Leonid Sykiäinen, Levent Baştürk, Magnus Berg, Marcia Hermansen, Margaret J. Rauch, Maria Küchen, Marika Palmblad, Mehmet Ali Aslan, Muammer Kadal, Mustafa Gezen, Oliver Leaman, Ömer Eken, Örjan Strandberg, Ozan Oyarkılıçgil, Özcan Keleş, Patrik Hällzon, Selçuk Akti, Şerafettin Pektaş, Shantikumar Hettiarachchi, Simon Shamoun, Susan Chandler, Süveyda Karakaya, Thomas Michel, Victoria Clement, and to Yusuf Alan for careful editing, and to Anna Weil for making my efforts at English more intelligible without losing my tone. Many thanks to all the people that have sown small seeds that in the end changed me. Hjärtligt tack!/Çok teşekkür ederim!

Index